1.·35

STORIES

FROM HOLY WRIT

Dulcissimae

et

Carissimae

HELEN WADDELL

STORIES

from

HOLY WRIT

The Macmillan Company

NEW YORK · 1950

*Printed in the United States of America
By The Haddon Craftsmen, Inc., Scranton, Pa.*

NOTE

THESE stories were written during the six years between 1914 and 1920, for a small missionary magazine called *Daybreak:* its editors were George Wilson of India and A. R. Crawford of Manchuria, where my own father had been a pioneer missionary. The earlier stories had already been told to the two small nephews and the smaller niece whose names, to their great embarrassment, appeared in the first number: Jack, I remember, was found scoring his name out with a furious stubby pencil. These were the children who discovered Pharaoh's palace in the white-painted beehive, and for whom the huge umbrella that covered the pony trap was Abraham's tent at Hebron. The background was an old whitewashed house in County Down, its three foot thickness of wall sunk in ivy and in apple orchards, but with the silence of the bog behind it, where at night one could sometimes hear the drumming of the snipe.

The later stories, beginning with the story of Saul the King, were also written for *Daybreak,* and for children, but they are graver and sadder. In those years I was nursing my invalid stepmother in a thin red brick house in Belfast. It was on its doorstep that I found the little shabby dog whose story is the foreword to this book. He does not belong to Holy Writ, but he was perhaps the reason why all the other stories were written.

They were never collected to be published in book form, because in the years between I grew impatient of any tampering with the austerity of the Authorised Version. But the generation for which they were written is now itself the older generation, and importunate that their children shall have the stories which were read to themselves, more than thirty years ago: and one grows old and indulgent, even to the prose of one's youth.

Kilmacrew, County Down, 1914:   HELEN WADDELL
Primrose Hill, Hampstead, 1949

About a Dog

HE WAS a shabby little dog, and he was thin. He was sitting on the doorstep when I came down one morning, very early, before anyone was up. I think he had been there all night. But he jumped up when the door opened, very hurriedly, and trotted a little way down the path, and then he stopped and turned round and looked at me with big frightened eyes, and began wagging his tail. He did not wag it very hard, because he was so afraid that he was going to be scolded for sitting there, and he didn't dare to say much. But he wagged it a little, because he had just a faint hope that whoever opened the door would not be cross with him, and he did want somebody to like him a little. He had such imploring eyes that it hurt to look at them; and when I got down on my knees beside him and patted his untidy little head he gave a little choked bark that was half a whine, and the tail wagged so hard that all the small body seemed wagging too. But he still looked at me, and his eyes were very hungry. So I said, "Wait, Doggie, till I get you something to eat," and he sat down and thumped his tail up and down on the tiles, and I ran into the house. I was not more than two minutes, but coming back I thought I heard a yelp, and when I got to the door the milk boy was standing there grinning, and away, away down the road I saw a little dog running as hard as it could go. The milk boy hadn't meant to be nasty; he said he was a dirty wee beast, and he had just kicked him out of that; he thought we wouldn't want him about the place. I hoped all morning that he would come back; I could not get him out of my head, the eager eyes of him, and the nervous little tail. But he never came back.

That was years ago, and every now and then I remember him, and it hurts even yet. I remembered him only yesterday, and then I began thinking how queer it was that one should care so much, just in a minute, for a little strange dog; and from that I began thinking that if we could really feel that God cared as much about us, if it were only for five minutes out of our whole lives, as I had cared about a little dog, it would make all the difference.

Of course, we know it says in the Bible that God likes us, that He cares what becomes of us, and that when we are sorry He is sorry and when we are glad He is glad. But it is hard to take it in. There are so many people for Him to think about: the people in your own house and the milk boy and the people next door, and the people in the trains and the tram man and the boys who sell the papers—all the people you can see, and all the people you can't see; the little black children in the missionary pictures and all their fathers and mothers. He has to go round so many, He can't possibly care, really care, about each one of us. If there were only you, He might possibly care the way your father cares, but when you have to share Him with so many it seems to send Him farther and farther away. It talks in the Bible about His taking you under His wings, and at first it sounds as if you had a warm roof all to yourself, but when you think of all the other people, the roof seems to stretch bigger and bigger and higher and higher till it is as far away as the sky, and the rain and the wind can get at you, and it makes no difference to the roof; it is too far away.

But there is one word in the Catechism that makes it easier. Do you remember where it says, "God is infinite"? It is a hard word, but what it really means is just this, that God is very big—bigger than you can even think. He is so big that there is enough of Him for everybody. So instead of thinking of the crowds and crowds of people He has to care about, just think how very, very big His heart must be. I nearly broke my heart for a little dog that I only saw for a minute, and if I could care as much as that, think how much tenderness there must be in God. I did not keep on fretting about him; other things put him out of my head. But if I had had a bigger heart I wouldn't have forgotten. And God is so much bigger that He can care for far more people, and so much kinder that He can care much harder. He is like the sea: you can fill buckets and buckets, and there is just as much left as when you began. Only He is bigger and kinder than the sea.

So the next time you are afraid about anything, and the next time you are vexed with yourself and think you are so horrid nobody could like you much, and the next time you feel lonely and out of things, remember that God cares, cares what becomes of you, and cares terribly—far, far more than you would care for a little hungry dog.

CONTENTS

Note v

Foreword: About a Dog vii

It Happened in Egypt 3

Joseph and His Brethren 11

The Story of Jacob the Supplanter 53

The Story of Saul the King 97

The Building of the Wall 153

"Nineveh, that Great City" 185

"The Star which they saw in the East" 191

Matthew the Publican 195

A Man of the Pharisees 203

"For He had Great Possessions" 211

Lazarus of Bethany 217

"There came also Nicodemus" 223

"A Young Man whose Name was Saul" 229

"After these things Paul . . . came to Corinth" 235

"After two years, Felix . . . left Paul bound" 241

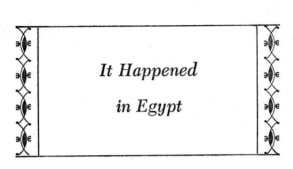

It Happened

in Egypt

ONE

STEPHEN is seven, and Jack is five, and Sara is three and a half, and mostly digging with a spoon. But we were all lying on the grass one Sunday afternoon, and Stephen wanted a story. He really wanted "Ali Baba and the Forty Thieves," because a big tree had been uprooted and there was a good robber's cave underneath; but I said it was Sunday and he would have to do with Moses in the Bulrushes, only we would do it a new way. So we lay quite flat—you would wonder how different things look when your eyes are very close to the ground. It is too wet to lie on the grass now, but try it on the carpet the next time somebody is telling you a story, and you will see all sorts of houses and bridges and caves underneath the chairs. There was a stream through the grass where we were lying, a very little one, with rushes. But looking at it this way it was very big, and the rushes were higher than our heads, which is just what bulrushes should be. "Now," I said, "this is the land of Egypt, and it's very sunny and very hot, and that's the river Nile. Where's the house where Moses' father and mother lived?" Jack found it. It was a big stone near the river, so that Moses' mother would not have very far to carry the water. "And where's the big white palace where Pharaoh lived?" "There!" shrieked Stephen. It was the wooden house where the bees live, but it was painted white, and it glistened like white marble in the sun, and the big brown and yellow bees walking up and down were Pharaoh's fat sentries. So then I told about the proud cruel King who lived inside it, and how he hated the Hebrews—that is what Moses' father and mother were, just as your father is an Irishman—and how he ordered all their little baby boys to be thrown into the river. So when Moses was born in the dark little

[3]

house by the Nile, they did not know what to do. His mother couldn't bear to take him and throw him into the river for the crocodiles to eat, for he had such a nice face, and so she tried to hide him. But three months went by, and the baby grew big and began to cry very loud, and she was afraid that one of the fat brown sentries would hear him, and tell. So she went and gathered the bulrushes from the river behind her house— we could see them—and made them into a basket, and tarred it all over so that the water couldn't get in, and made it like a little soft nest and put the boy in it, and then set it into the river, not where the water was running, but among the rushes, so that it couldn't drift away. We chose the exact clump of rushes, a good thick clump, because Miriam, who was his big sister, wanted to hide behind them and see what would happen. We watched too for a while, and when a frog hopped into the water Jack squealed that it was a crocodile, and we threw stones at it to keep it away from Moses' bulrushes.

It was a very hot day, and inside the big white palace there was no air at all, and the black slaves walked up and down sprinkling water on the floors. The Princess, Pharaoh's daughter, got hotter and hotter, and at last she said she would go down to the river and have a bathe. We saw her coming down from the house, because there was a big yellow dandelion, and that was her sun umbrella. One of her slaves carried it, and another one fanned her with a fan of peacock's feathers. They walked along by the bank, looking for a place with nice clear water and yellow sand to paddle in, when the Princess stopped and said, "What's that?" It was poor little Moses all alone and shrieking, just the way Sara used to do, when she wanted her bottle. ["Did not," said Sara.] So they all hunted about, and at last the Princess saw something dark in the middle of the rushes, like a bird's nest in the hedge, and one of the maids gathered up her long skirts and waded in. She didn't like it at all, for she was afraid something would nip at her toes, but she got the basket and waded back, and the Princess lifted the lid, and there was the poor baby with his face all puckered up and crying dreadfully. The Princess hardly knew what to do, for she didn't know much about babies, but she picked him up and hugged him and said soft things to him, and Moses stopped crying, for he thought he was going to get something to eat, and he chuckled when she danced him up and down. He had such a nice face when he laughed that the Princess made up her mind there and then that she would take him for her own baby; she guessed that he must be one of the poor little thrown-out Hebrew babies, but she knew that she could easily get round her father. But meantime the baby was hungry. And just as he was beginning to howl again, little Miriam stepped out from behind the rushes and said, "Please, shall I go and get a Hebrew woman to nurse him for you?" and the Princess said, "Go." So Miriam ran home to the little dark house, and told her mother all about it, and to come quick, for Moses was crying so hard. You can just imagine how the mother ran. Somehow I think the Princess suspected who she was, but she was a kind Princess and pretended she didn't. She just told her to take the baby and nurse him for her, and she would pay her for nursing him until he was old enough to come and live in the palace. So Miriam and the baby and the mother went back to the little dark house, and the Princess and her maids and the sun umbrella and the fan of the peacock's feathers went back to the big white palace, and the fat brown sentries went on marching up and down.

And I'll tell you the rest of it next time.

T W O

DO YOU remember, we were lying beside the Nile, and watching the Princess walking back to the palace, and Moses' mother carrying him home? Well, Moses stayed in the little dark house till he was old enough to run about by himself, and now and then the Princess came walking down the river path under the sun umbrella, and brought him sweets and played with him. Then came a day that the Princess said, "I think he is big enough to do without a nurse now. I want him myself. Bring him up to the palace to-morrow." So his mother put on his best clothes and brushed his hair and walked holding his hand up the river path, and past the fat brown sentries, and into the palace, but she was trying not to cry all the way. The Princess was looking out for him, and she had two toy oxen for him to play with, and a tray full of cakes and sweets, sticky ones, and Moses sat down on the floor, and when he wasn't looking, the Princess signed to his mother and she slipped away. And when Moses lifted his head, he was all alone in a great rich room with silk cushions on the marble floor, and a fountain in the middle with goldfish swimming in the basin, and great ladies in long trailing dresses, instead of the little dark kitchen, and the comfortable smell of the earthen floor, and Miriam and his mother, and the sand outside the door. He dropped the toy oxen, and he shut his eyes and he cried. The Princess was as nice to him as she could be: she took him on her knee and petted him, and her maids pretended to play crocodiles and gobble each other up; and after a while he stopped crying. But he never forgot. He lived with the Princess just as if he were her son and a Prince himself, and the sentries let him play with their swords, and everybody was kind to him. The Princess wanted him to forget. She wanted him to live always at the palace and be a great Egyptian Prince. But he never forgot. He knew that the people who lived in the little dark huts by the river and worked like slaves, the people that the Egyptians oppressed, were his people, and their God his God. He grew to be a man, tall and strong and splendid, though always slow of speech, and he had learned all the wisdom of the East. But always he was waiting and watching to see what he could do for his people.

There came a day that Moses went for a walk to watch the men building the Pyramids. And as he stood he saw an old Hebrew slave tugging at a great stone. It slipped just as he got it into place, and fell with a crash, and in a flash, the overseer —a big Egyptian—came down on him with his whip. Now Moses had a very soft heart, and the cruelty of it drove him mad. He made for the overseer and struck him on the head, and the man dropped at his feet. He had killed him. Moses buried the body in the sand and stole back to the palace. He had killed a man for being cruel: and what had he been himself? The next day he found out that he had been seen: and he was afraid. And indeed, when the old King heard of it he was in great anger, and Moses had to creep out of the palace by night, and fly to the Desert for his life.

A tennis lawn makes a good Desert, when the grass is very dry and very hot. But we took the lane to the Moss Field, because at the end of it you come to a well. As far as you can see in the Desert there is nothing but sand, and miles away a little green speck with a pool of water and some palm trees. The sun blazes down on it all day, and at night the moon shines in a sky so blue that it is black, and there is hardly a living thing stirring but two lions maybe, and sometimes a caravan. This was the Desert that Moses had to cross alone. He took a water-bottle with him, and raisins and figs, and dates—as much as he could carry, for there are no houses in the Desert. And he wandered for days and days. We crawled down the dry, hot lane very slowly, Stephen and Jack and Sara and I, and the sun baked us. And we hadn't any raisins, or figs, or dates.

It came near sunset. Moses had eaten all his raisins. He had filled his bottle at a little pool that morning, but it was all gone by mid-day, and now there was no water anywhere. Away on the sky line he saw blue mountains, and he said to himself, "Those are the mountains of Midian," and hurried on, for where there are mountains there will be valleys and running water, and green grass. He went on and on, dizzy with heat, and thirst, and tiredness, and at last he saw the first palm trees, and we came to the well. It is an old well with stone steps leading down to it, and trails of grass hanging over it, and a damp green smell. The water was very low in it, but he tied his bottle to his girdle and lowered it down, and had a long, long drink.

I had to hurry the rest of it; how he lay and rested, and how the seven daughters of the Priest of Midian came to water their father's sheep. And how some rough herdsmen frightened them and tried to chase them away, and Moses jumped up and laid about him till they took to their heels, and then came back and drew the water for the sheep. And how they brought him home with them to their father's house, and how he fell in love with one of them—"And married her and lived happy ever after"—said Stephen, who knows how all stories end—"And that's the end."

He did marry her. And he lived in the old house in Midian for forty years, and shepherded his father-in-law's sheep, and was likely happy enough, except when he remembered the great things he had meant to do for his people. But it was not the end. It was only the beginning. Even if you have broken your life and made a mess of it the way Moses did, God gives you a fresh start. Moses had to wait forty years for it. But when it came, he did what he had dreamed. He set his people free.

Joseph and

His Brethren

ONE

THIS is a story that ends in Egypt, but it does not begin there. It begins more than a hundred years before Moses was found in the bulrushes: and it began with an old oak tree at Hebron in Palestine and in a big black tent.

[The tree we had was a beech, but it doesn't matter: it was on a mound in the Moss Field, with short dry grass, and the wind always blows there, just as it used to blow on Abraham's face when he came to sit at his tent door in the evening and watch the sun going down. And our tent was only a big black umbrella, but it covered us all if we sat very tight.]

It was an old tent, for first of all Abraham had lived here, and then his son Isaac, and now it was Isaac's son Jacob. Jacob had been in foreign parts nearly all his life, but when he was old he came back to the old oak and the old tent, and settled down. But there was a crowd of little tents round it now, for he had twelve sons, and herds and herds of cows and sheep and goats. But at the time this story begins it was very quiet in the big black tent, for ten of the older ones were away, and the only two at home were Joseph and a very little one called Benjamin. Joseph was the son that his father liked best, except of course for Benjamin: but then everyone loved Benjamin, he was so fat and so small, tumbling about like a puppy. Even the big brothers, who were a very tough lot, liked Benjamin. But they hated Joseph: he was their stepbrother, and his father's favourite, and they jeered at him for his good manners and his pride and his queer, dreamy ways. They thought he was a conceited cub, and it made things worse when their father gave him a coat that was all bright colours. They were always teasing him and making fun of him, and Joseph was not sorry when the whole ten cleared off early one morning with droves and droves and droves of sheep to graze them on the green fields of Shechem, for the grass round Hebron was now all trampled and bare. There was a mountain between called Gerizim, rocky and barren, but on the other side of it the grass was green and deep.

So the days went by, and the old man began to wonder how the boys were, for he had a heart for them all. It seemed very quiet, with nobody shouting and laughing and chasing. So, in the end he called Joseph and told him he wanted him to go and find his brothers: he need not stay, just see how they all were, and if the sheep were getting fat, and bring word home. So Joseph put some dates and cheese and bread in his wallet and said good-bye and started off, only Benjamin said he wanted to go too and started running after him on his fat legs and tumbled down, and had to be picked up and carried home again. And the old man took him in his arms and said Benjamin must stay and keep him company, so the two of them stood watching Joseph go down the valley as far as they could see, and then Jacob went back into the old black tent and Benjamin began digging wells with a sharp stick.

It was a long way to Shechem. Joseph slept under a tree one night and the next night in a cave, but at last he saw the steep rocks of Gerizim in front of him, and knew the green fields of Shechem would be on the other side. You can imagine how he would hurry the last bit of the way, for even if he was a little afraid of his brothers, it was a very long time since he had seen them, and it is very lonesome tramping all by yourself for days on a hill road. And there was always Reuben, he thought. Reuben was kind, especially if none of the others were about. Odd, thought Joseph, Reuben was the eldest, but he always seemed a little afraid of the others: hated being laughed at for being soft. It was getting dark now, as he climbed the hill: soon he would be at the top and would look down and see the glimmer of their camp fires and hear the bleating of the sheep. And he thought of the smell of the meat roasting over the fire, and the hot baked bread, and wondered if Reuben would take him to sleep with him. He hoped it would be Reuben.

By this time he had got to the ridge of the hill, and he stopped and looked. He could see the fields for miles, but they were dark and quiet, never a glimmer of fire or a bleat from a sheep, just the quiet of the hills and the coming of night. He couldn't believe it: he hurried down the mountainside, and tramped up and down, shouting and whistling, and just as he had given up hope a man came to him over the darkening fields.

"What have you lost?" said he.

"I am looking for my brothers," said Joseph. "They were grazing their sheep. Please, did you see them anywhere?"

"They went away out of this," said the man, "but I heard them say they were going on to Dothan."

Joseph's face fell. "Is it far?" said he. "It is the better part of ten miles," said the man. "But let you come home with me and have bite and sup, and I'll put you on the road in the morning."

And with that he took Joseph home to his tent, and brought him a bowl of milk, but before Joseph had finished it he was fast asleep. And next morning he started off early, early, before the dew was dry on the grass, with a handful of dates in his pocket, and the kind man told him the way and said with any luck he would be there by dinner time.

"They'll be glad to see you," said he.

But Joseph was not so sure.

TWO

JOSEPH'S big brothers had been very busy all morning, but now they were lying on the grass and waiting till dinner was ready. And suddenly one of them said, "What's that?" And they all got up and looked, and away, away on the hot white road they saw a little speck moving. It was such a lonely country that they couldn't think who it would be, and they watched while the speck drew nearer, and then the one with the sharpest eyes saw that it was someone in a bright coloured coat, and said with his sneering laugh, "Here's the dreamer coming." They stood and watched him trudging up the road, very far away, and you would think that they might have been sorry for the young brother tramping so far to find them all by himself. But the old jealousy leaped up in them, like the flames when you put the poker into the fire, and it burned all the pity out of them. They thought of all the times their father had thrashed them when he found them hurting him, and all the ways he had that they hated, and they said, "Now's our chance to pay him out. We'll kill him, and throw him into a pit, and tell our father a lion must have killed him somewhere on the road. And we'll see what becomes of his dreams."

Now Reuben had always a liking for Joseph, but he was not brave enough to stand up against all the rest. So he said, "Don't kill him yourselves, whatever you do. Throw him into that old pit there, and leave him, but don't touch him yourselves."

And then he went off somewhere by himself, for he didn't want to be there when the poor lad came up, and hear the rest jeering at him and him crying when they threw him into the pit. Reuben was soft-hearted, but a terrible coward; he was planning to himself that when all the rest were asleep he would go to the pit, and pull his small brother up, and start him off on the road home, before any of them were stirring.

By this time Joseph was nearly at the tents. You can guess how his heart died in him when he saw the look on the faces of the nine big brothers waiting for him. They took him, and they tore the bright coat off him, and dragged him over the grass away to that pit, and dropped him into it. There used to be water in it in the time of the rains, but now in the summer it was dry. And there they left him, and went back to their dinner. And Joseph sat on the sand at the bottom of the pit, and looked up at the ring of blue sky away at the top, and wondered how long it would be before he died.

They were just in the middle of dinner when one of them happened to raise his head, and there—they had never heard it coming, for the camels make no noise on the sand—there was a caravan coming down the road, camels and camels and camels padding along, with great loads swagging on either side of their humps, spices and balm and sweet smelling things, and men driving them, dark-skinned men with fierce black eyes and long sharp knives in their belts, and great white turbans. They were going on down through Palestine, and away across the Desert, and so into Egypt, and there they would sell the spices and the balm: the very scents that the Princess in Pharaoh's palace would sprinkle about her room and pour into her bath. The brothers stood and watched them swinging past, and suddenly Judah spoke out.

"What's the use," he said, "of letting that small boy die? It will do us no good. Let's sell him instead to these foreigners. After all, he's our brother."

It wasn't much kinder than the killing, for often the little slave boys had a bad time; but there was a chance that he might get a kind master who would keep him to wait on him at table and fan him when he went to sleep. And I think after all Judah meant well. So in a minute or two Joseph heard steps and voices coming to the top of the pit, and a face looked down at him, and someone let down a rope and told him to hold tight, and they hauled him up into the sunlight again. At first he was glad, but they hurried him over the grass to where the big dark-skinned men stood, and he heard them wrangling about the price of something, and suddenly it flashed on him that the thing they were selling was himself. He turned to his brothers and he clung to them; long years after they remembered how he had clung to them and how terribly he cried, but it was too late then. Now they laughed at him; the price was settled for twenty pieces of silver—do you remember Who it was that was sold for thirty?—and Joseph was tied and flung on one of the camels on top of the bales of spices, and away the caravan swung on its way to the Desert, and the big brothers sat down to finish their dinner, and squabble over dividing the money.

And Reuben? Reuben came home about sunset and slipped quietly over to the pit without seeing any of them, and looked down. He could see nothing. He called "Joseph! are you there?" and his own voice came back to him hollow. He had come too late. He rushed back to the tents wild with grief, and when they told him what they had done, he wasn't much better, for he was wondering how he would ever face his father. Then— it was a cruel thing to do—they took the gay little coat and dabbled it with blood from a kid that they had killed, and when they came back to the old black tent under the oak, and old Jacob came out to meet them, and asked where was Joseph, they showed him the little blood-stained coat. "We found this," they said. "Look at it and see if it is your son's coat or not." You see, they would not even say "our brother." The old man looked and knew it and cried out with a great cry. It was Joseph's coat. He was dead. Joseph, his son, had been torn in pieces in the wilderness. For days he cried for him. It says that his sons tried to comfort him; I suppose they were sorry when they saw how terribly they had hurt him. But it was too late. They would go to bed at night and hear the old man crying in the tent be-side theirs, and remember how Joseph had caught their knees and cried while they were selling him. But it was too late. The camels were hundreds of miles away, swinging across the desert.

I'll tell you the rest again: how they meant it for evil, and God turned it to good. But I want you now to think how it all began: just little brothers fighting among themselves, and sulking be-cause one got nicer things than the others.

THREE

HAVE you an old war map in your house, a big one with North Africa on it, and the blue Mediterranean Sea? I want you to get it and find the Suez Canal, where the great liners go up and down. It is a sort of watergate between the East and the West, the West where you and the French and the Spanish and the Italians live, and the East with Arabia and India and China and Burma and Malaya and Japan.

Have you found it yet? If you look, you will see a black streak of water, and great stretches of desert on either side. Now shut your eyes and think away back to a time before the Canal was dug, when there was no deep black line of water like the trenches in the bog, and the desert lay in one great sweep from Palestine to Egypt. It is quiet enough even now, for the great ships make no noise and the water is very still.

But it was far quieter then, when only the caravans came swinging across the desert, and quietest of all at night, when Joseph lay awake beside the man who drove his camel—he used to give him a corner of his blanket—and the quiet stars shone down on the quiet sand. Joseph used to lie and watch the moon coming up over the desert, and listened till his ears ached with the silence. At home, under the old oak tree at Hebron, there was always something stirring, but here there was not any sound at all, except when a jackal howled out in the dark beyond the camp fire, or when one of the camels coughed in his sleep. Joseph used to lie awake and think. At first he could not, for the memory of his brothers was like a flame that seemed to burn him, and his anger turned him sick. But after a while he quieted down, and began to wonder why it was that they had hated him so. They were a bad lot, he knew that, but they didn't

hate little Benjamin the way they hated him. Could it possibly
be something in himself? It was a very long time before Joseph
would give in to that. He knew that they thought he was conceited, and proud of being his father's pet, and that he gave
himself airs. He had not meant to; but it was a very dismal surprise to Joseph, as it is to most of us, to find that you can be
very nasty without meaning to; that unless you give your mind
to being kind to everybody, you will very likely be cruel to
somebody.

Joseph did not like finding himself out, but it was good for
him. He did not like himself much now, and it made him readier
to like other people. He began first with the Midianites, and he
found they were oddly kind to him, in spite of their fierce eyes
and glittering knives. The one thing he was afraid of now was
the master to whom he knew they were going to sell him. The
time was drawing very near. They had left the sand of the desert,
and were going along through green fields, with palm trees by
the road—grass so green that it reminded Joseph of the fields
round Hebron in the spring. The man who drove his camel told
Joseph that it was the land of Goshen, and the best land in
Egypt; and "there," he said, pointing to a great cluster of palms
and a gleam of white stone, "there is the City of the Sun."

They camped that night outside the city walls, but early in
the morning they were astir, for they wanted a good place in
the market-square. All the bales of sweet spices and frankincense and myrrh they piled up, and when the sun grew hot the
whole square was fragrant with the perfumes that had come
from Syria. There were plenty of buyers: all the drug-sellers in
the City of the Sun were swarming like bees round the Midianites, wrangling and chaffing, and Joseph sat on an upturned cask
and looked at the strange faces, and wondered if he would ever
understand the strange words they used. Then a sudden silence
fell, and he looked round, and the crowd had scattered, and the
men who had brought him were on their faces uttering saluta-

tions, and there before him stood a splendid figure, stately and indifferent and kind. It was the Captain of Pharaoh's Guard. He was passing through the square on his way home and smelt the perfumes, and remembered that his very pretty wife was scolding that morning because she had no scent for her bath. So he stopped to buy her white jars of spikenard, and as he spoke his eyes fell on a fair-skinned boy among the black Midianite merchants, a handsome boy with great eyes staring at him, for never in his life had Joseph seen anything so magnificent as Potiphar, the Captain of Pharaoh's Guard.

FOUR

Do YOU remember, it was getting near sunset, and the Captain of Pharaoh's Guard had given the word for the night to the sentries, and was going home to dine? And passing through the market-square he had smelt the perfumes from the great bales piled up in the corner, and remembered that he must buy spikenard for his wife, and stopped, and his eye had fallen on Joseph. And when I left off last time he and Joseph were looking at each other face to face, and the Midianite merchants had their foreheads touching the ground. Joseph should have been flat on his face too, but he was not used to being a slave; the Syrian shepherds, who were his people, were not afraid of any man, or beast either, and, anyway, the Captain of the Guard was so magnificent that Joseph could only sit still and stare. He liked beautiful things, and the Captain of the Guard, standing there in the red sunset, blazed like a great bright jewel, flashing points of light from the gold in his head-dress, and the sword at his side, and the chain that Pharaoh had put round his neck with his own hand. I don't think he minded that Joseph hadn't grovelled before him; and when at last Joseph remembered his manners and slid off the cask to his feet (for it isn't polite to sit still when older people than you are standing), the Captain smiled at him, for he saw the wonder in Joseph's eyes.

"And where do *you* come from?" he asked. He spoke in Egyptian and Joseph didn't understand and he shook his head, but he knew the voice was kindly, and he smiled back. Potiphar liked the quick way he had sprung to the ground, and he liked the way the boy carried his head, and he liked the way he smiled. Then he turned to the sprawling Midianites and said, not quite so kindly, "Is the boy for sale? Get up!"

[21]

It was not five minutes before the bargain was struck and Joseph handed over. Potiphar had to pay dear for him, but he did not mind what he paid for a thing once he had set his heart on it. And off they swung, two soldiers of the Guard in front with drawn swords, then Potiphar alone, and Joseph a step or two behind.

They were just leaving the market-square when Potiphar suddenly stopped and blessed himself. He had clean forgotten the jars of spikenard he had stopped to buy for his young wife, and he chuckled to himself as he thought how she would have sulked. Then he turned to Joseph and said something, still in Egyptian, and held up his five fingers and tossed him a gold piece. Joseph had learned the Egyptian for spikenard for he had heard the drugsellers squabbling over the price of it all day in the square, and he guessed from the five fingers that he was to get five jars. So he caught the gold piece and ran, and Potiphar marched on and watched the sun going down. It seemed no time till he heard bare feet pattering after him, and when he looked round his small slave was trotting behind him, with the five white jars and his hand held out. Potiphar had forgotten that there was any change, but he nodded very good-humouredly, and slipped the money into his pocket without even glancing at it to count it. But that was Potiphar's way.

Have you bricks that you sometimes play with? For just here you might build Potiphar's house, where Joseph was to live for years and years. Dominoes will do beautifully for the floor, for you want a marble floor, black and white, with pillars here and there (draughtsmen make nice, round pillars, and they are black and white, too). And if you can get chess-men, black and white —the ones that look like horses' heads—they will do for statues, for the things the Egyptians drew are very like our chess-men. And right in the middle of the inner room a glass salt-cellar will make a splendid crystal basin. Potiphar's wife used to lie beside it and play with the goldfishes, and it was so cool and clear and deep that when it grew breathlessly hot, she would dive in herself, and pretend she was a goldfish too. And then she would empty one of her jars of perfume into the water, and when the poor little goldfish died in the poisoned water, she only laughed and said she was teaching them to float. For she was a cruel woman, although she was very beautiful. And how cruel she was to something other than goldfish I'll tell you next time.

FIVE

IT WAS a very hot day. Ever since early morning Joseph had been up and about in the fields, visiting the stables, watching the vine-dressers in the vineyard, measuring the depth of the water in the great fish ponds in the garden of Potiphar's house (for water in Egypt dries up quickly), setting each man to his work, and listening to their stories against each other with a patience that was endless. The slaves loved him, though he was their master. For Joseph was not any longer the small ragged slave of the market-place. That was years and years ago. Now he was a man, and every year the Captain of the Guard liked him better and believed in him more, until, as Joseph said himself, "My master knoweth not what is with me in the house, and he hath committed all that he hath to my hand." Potiphar used to watch his new slave. He liked to have him near him, liked to have him fill his wine-cup at dinner, and pour the water over his hands, and fan him to sleep. It was not only that he did not drop things, and did not tell lies, and was always there when you wanted him. There was a curious charm about him, a sort of transparent shining. He was different from other people. When Potiphar came home after the dust and clamour of the guard-room and the barracks—even after the drowsy, rich perfumes that hung about his wife's room, he used to think Joseph was like the freshness of the fields. He could not understand it for a long time; at last he said, "It must be the grace of God."

That, you remember, is what Joseph had not in the old days, under the big black tent. He was honest, but he was not gracious. He used to carry his head very high, and when your chin is very high in the air, you will sometimes tramp on other people's toes. Then that terrible thing happened to Joseph himself, and he was so badly hurt that he grew afraid of hurting others. Besides, away from his own people, Joseph had nobody to talk to but God. Nobody else spoke his language. When you think of it, God is the only person who understands everybody's language. And it was good for Joseph. David said once, "Thy gentleness hath made me great." It was God's gentleness that made Joseph great, and taught him gentleness too.

So this was how it was that Joseph had spent the morning going all over the estate. Potiphar was big, and careless, and generous, and he threw everything into Joseph's hands. "He knew not aught he had save the bread that he did eat." And the wonderful thing was that whatever Joseph put his hand to prospered. You know there are people who can grow clumps of sweet violets where other people could hardly grow grass. There is a virtue goes out of them, and Joseph had it. The very grapes from the vineyard on the hill were finer, and the corn richer in the fields. And he himself had grown so good to look on that there are old Persian poems written about his beauty, and men read them even to-day. Once again Joseph was in danger of carrying his head very high. And once again a cloud came over the sun, and he was thrown into a dark place.

As I was telling you, it was very hot. It was just that breathless time in the afternoon when the dogs lie asleep in the sun, and the doves tuck their heads under their wings, and there is no chirp from the birds. Joseph came in from the blazing courtyard into the great dim house, and down long corridors of cool marble, with the soft splash of water from the fountain in his ears. The house was very still, for all the slaves were at their work outside. He passed on steadily to his own room; for there were long accounts to be made up every day, and overseers were very exact in ancient Egypt. And then, above the splash of the fountain, he heard someone calling his name.

It was the voice of his mistress, and he obeyed her and went but, as he went, he was afraid. He had seen her first the evening

Potiphar brought him home barefoot at his heels, and in the soft dusk of her room she had seemed to him like the first great star that comes into the sky after sunset. But even then she made him ill at ease, for there was something sinister about her, as if her beauty were the beauty of a snake. Always she was her most charming to him, but he feared her, for as he grew older, he saw that there was no honour in her. As much as he could he kept out of her way, but he could not avoid her altogether, because she was his master's wife, and Potiphar loved her.

She was beautiful but there was no shame in her. When Joseph came to her she told him that she cared for him—cared for him more than for the great Egyptian who was her husband. And then she prayed him to love her in return, and together they would deceive him. It was enough to turn Joseph's head to be told these things by a woman who had been set high above him like a star, but his answer is one of the finest things in the world. "Behold, my master hath given all that he hath into my hand, neither hath he kept anything back from me save thee, because thou art his wife. How then can I do this great wickedness and sin against God?" And with that he turned from her and went out.

Her anger was terrible. For she was beautiful, and proud of her beauty, and when she found that she could not make him care for her she wanted only one thing and that was to punish him. And so when Potiphar came home that night he found her pacing up and down her room in a frenzy, and she turned on him.

"See," she cried, "that Hebrew slave that you make so much of! He came into the house this day and insulted me—me, your wife. And when I cried out, he fled."

Potiphar would not believe her at first, but at last she goaded him into believing that Joseph was not what he had thought him —that he had been monstrously deceived. And a great gale of anger came on him, and he sent for Joseph, but Joseph would say nothing, for he would not speak against a woman. Then Potiphar clapped his hands, and two soldiers of the guard came in and took Joseph between them. And once again he went out with two soldiers of the guard at sunset, down the steps that he had climbed behind them, a little bare-footed slave, so many years ago, now a prisoner in bonds. And this time he never came back.

SIX

IT WAS sunset; and Joseph went out from the presence of the Captain of the Guard, bound, between two soldiers. He was going to the King's Prison. And that night, in the black dark of the dungeon, with chains on his hands and heavy fetters on his feet, there came a terrible darkness on his soul. He could not believe that only that afternoon he had been walking in the sun. It seemed so long ago; so long ago since he came through the sunny courtyard and into the quiet house, with the splash of the fountain in his ears. Coming through the court the slaves had bowed before him: he had come into the great house like its master, so sure of himself, so sure of his good name. And now he was an outcast slave, a poor prisoner, glad if a dog would lick his hand. There was nobody to care what became of him. The man whom he cared for most in the world, the great Egyptian who had been his master, had turned against him, had believed that he had betrayed him. That hurt most of all. And it was all because he had tried to keep faith.

Joseph never forgot that night in prison. Long after, someone wrote a psalm about him, and told how they "afflicted his feet with fetters," put heavy chains upon him; and then—it is one of the strangest lines ever written—"the iron entered into his soul." It is not so hard a thing to have iron on one's flesh. Thousands of years after, Paul and Silas lay in a dungeon at Philippi, and they cared so little about their chains that they were singing. But then they felt that the Lord Christ was with them; while Joseph —it seemed to him that God had forgotten him. He had gone away and left him, and there was no one to care for his soul. It did not matter whether you tried to be good or not. God did not care. The beautiful woman who had tempted him was safe and petted and cared for, fast asleep now and happy; and he was out in the dark, chained like a dog. He had been a fool to think God cared what you did. He did not care any more than if you were a fly buzzing on a windowpane. He did not care what happened to you. He was cruel. The chains had come very near Joseph's soul.

And then something happened. I wonder if you remember a story about a prison, long after, where Peter lay asleep, chained between two soldiers; how an angel came and touched the chains, and they fell off, and he stood up free. That is what happened here. Joseph saw no angel, and the chains did not fall off his hands. But God Himself came and touched the crueller chains that were hurting his soul, and they dropped, and it was his soul that stood up free. The man who told the story in Hebrew long ago does not say very much about it; he only says, "The Lord shewed him kindness." But God's kindness is so wonderful a thing that if a man once gets a sight of it he never can forget. He did not tell Joseph why this cruel thing had happened to him. He did not even say that He would make it up to him. He only made him feel that He was there, that He had not forgotten, and Joseph's heart went out to Him in a great adoration. He did not care any more what chains were upon him, so long as he was God's.

The morning came, but it brought no deliverance. Day after day Joseph saw no face but the gaoler's, and it was not a very kind one. But even he noticed that Joseph was the only one of the prisoners who smiled at him and said "Thank you," when he dumped down the jug of water that had to do them for drinks all day. And one morning when he came in looking very ill, for he had a touch of fever, Joseph asked so kindly what was the matter with him, that the gaoler nearly dropped the jug in his surprise. And then he sat down and told Joseph all about it, at great length; he was so pleased to find that any of the prisoners cared about him at all. Then one day he came in with a mallet and a chisel and knocked off Joseph's chains, and told him to come his rounds with him and carry the water. And as time went on he trusted him more and more, till at last he gave the keys of the prison into his hand, and Joseph was left as much in charge as he had been in the old days with the Captain of the Guard. It was a change from being overseer of one of the greatest houses in Egypt to be warder in a dirty prison, and, in spite of all Joseph's patience, there were days when he sat looking through the prison bars into the ugly prison courtyard and thought of the other court, with its green palm trees and cool white marble, and the evenings when his master would saunter down to the fishponds, with his hand on his shoulder, and hear what he had been doing all day, and stop him in the middle of his accounts to look at a big carp under the rushes. They were good days, and Joseph wondered sometimes why God had spoiled his life.

We know now why it was, though Joseph did not. It was to make him fit to be overseer, not of the greatest house in Egypt, but of all Egypt itself. But it was years before Joseph knew, and the years were long years.

SEVEN

Dᴵᴰ you ever hear one of the saddest of the Hebrew proverbs —"Hope deferred maketh the heart sick?" That is what happened to some people in the days of the war, when someone they cared for was at the front, and the War Office wrote that he was missing, and morning after morning wore to evening and brought no word. It is not the quick sharp pain that would come if they knew he was killed; it is a slow sickness, and it is the hardest thing in the world to bear. God does not give it to many people, but He gave something like it to Joseph. You would think he had come through enough, that he had had so many hard things that he would never be very sure of himself again. But God is wise. The place that He was planning to give Joseph was so dangerous and so high that He could run no risks. It is like a man who is tempering a sword. Steel that is only for a dinner-knife might do with a little of the fire, but when it is for a sword that a man's life will depend on, it has to go into the furnace, and be hammered again and again. And so this heart-sickness came on Joseph that he might learn to steady his soul.

This is how it happened. You remember, Joseph was in charge of all the prisoners. Well, one day two men were brought in—two of the chief officers of Pharaoh's household, very fine and stately —the chief baker and the King's own cupbearer. Joseph was sorry for them, for he knew what it was like to be disgraced and put in prison after living in a great house, and he did his best to try and cheer them up. But one morning when he came in with their breakfasts, the two of them were sitting with their heads in their hands, looking so very wretched, that he set down the tray and asked what was the matter at all? And the cupbearer raised his head and said, "We had a wretched night; and we dreamt the

[31]

queerest dreams. We don't know what they mean, but we're afraid something awful is going to happen." "Tell me them," said Joseph. "God is the only person who knows what dreams mean, and maybe He will show me." The chief baker shook his head, for he had a bad conscience, and he was sure his dream meant no good; but the cupbearer was an honest, jolly soul and he plunged into his.

"I dreamt," he said, "that I saw a vine with three branches, and just while I was looking at it, green buds came on it, and then flowers, and before I knew there were big purple bunches of grapes. And it seemed to me Pharaoh's big gold drinking-cup was in my hand, and I squeezed the grapes into it with my fingers and gave it to the King just as I used to do." And Joseph said, "The three branches are three days. It means that in three days Pharaoh will send for you, and forget that he ever was angry, and you'll be standing behind him, and pouring out his wine just like the old days." And then suddenly, a great hope flashed into Joseph's mind. "And oh," he said, "when this happens and things are well with you, have me in your remembrance, and speak a word for me to Pharaoh, and bring me out of this house. Tell him that I was stolen away from my own country, and that I did nothing that they should put me in this dungeon." The cupbearer shook hands with him, for he was softhearted, and said, "Indeed I will." And at that the baker plucked up heart and said to himself, "Maybe I haven't been found out after all," and told his dream—a stranger one still—about carrying three baskets on his head, with cakes and buns for Pharaoh on top, and how the birds came and pecked at them. Joseph shook his head very sadly. "It is not so well for you," he said. "Pharaoh has not forgotten. In three days you will be hanged."

True enough, the third day after that was Pharaoh's birthday, and even the prison hung out a flag. Towards evening there came a thundering knock at the door—"Open in the King's name" —and the King's messenger handed in two letters. The governor of the prison opened the first, said, "Poor beggar!" and turned to two of the soldiers, and they took the chief baker out and hanged him. Then he opened the second, and it was a Royal pardon, and a command that the cupbearer should present himself at the palace at once; for Pharaoh was giving a great dinner that night, and he wanted his old servant behind his chair. The cupbearer had been in a great state all day, and now Joseph begged that he might go and tell him the good news. And he stayed with him, and helped him to pack, and brushed him up, and off he went beaming and vowing that he would speak to the King for Joseph that very night, and have him out in the morning. Joseph went to the gate to see him off, and stood looking after him as far as he could see, thinking he would maybe turn back and wave to him. But he did not, and Joseph turned in a little sadly. "But then," he said, "it's no wonder he was in a hurry. And if he speaks to the King to-night, word will come to-morrow. Who knows but this will be my last night in prison? To-morrow I'll be out in the sun, and I'll go to the market and hire out as a camel-driver in a caravan, and to-morrow night I shall be in the desert sleeping under the stars, and after that it won't be long till I see trees on the hill, and the old tent again." He could not sleep for thinking of it, and he thought morning would never come. But it did come, morning, and noon, and afternoon, and evening, and brought no word. "It will come to-morrow," said Joseph, and he lay down and tried to sleep. But it did not come to-morrow, nor to-morrow, nor to-morrow, until Joseph gave up hoping, and went about his work with the heart in him dead. The cupbearer had forgotten.

It might have made him bitter, but it did not. It only made him quiet and tolerant, and so patient. And it taught him that the only thing you can steady yourself on is God. I think Joseph must have said to himself every night—"My soul, wait thou only upon God."

EIGHT

IT WAS the night of the King's birthday that Joseph lay awake, expecting every minute to hear the thunder of the King's messenger at the door, and he did not come. A whole year went slowly round, and the great night came again, and once again the flags went up, and a small hope stirred in Joseph's heart. "Surely," he said, "the cupbearer will remember where he was this time last year, and will speak for me to Pharaoh." But he did not remember, and the night went by, and the year went by, and the great night came again. But this time there was no expectation in Joseph, only a great patience. He lay down and slept. And in the morning there came joy at last.

For that night Pharaoh slept ill, and when he did fall asleep it was to dream strange uneasy dreams. He dreamt that he was away from his palace, standing in deep grass beside the river bed. And seven big cows came splashing up from the river, nice fat cows, and began grazing beside him. And then seven thin ugly cows, evil-looking beasts, came up after them, and gobbled up the fat cows, and in his consternation Pharaoh awoke, and wondered what had made him dream anything so ugly. Then he turned on his pillow and fell asleep again. And no sooner was he over than he dreamed the same thing over again, but this time it was about seven yellow ears of corn, and seven ugly ones, black with the east wind, that ate them up. And once again he woke up and lay wide awake till morning. There was a great heaviness on him; he was certain that some great mischief was coming on himself or on his kingdom. And as soon as it was light, before even he had his breakfast, he sent for all the old wise men and magicians about the court, to ask them what was the meaning of his dreams. They stood before him in a row and stroked their shaven chins, and Pharaoh sat with his wine-cup untasted before him, and the fish cold on his plate, and stared at them with gloomy eyes. And one by one they said, "I give it up."

Suddenly the cupbearer gave a shout and clapped his hands to his head. Pharaoh turned round in sheer amazement, but the cupbearer was too much excited to notice. "I do remember my faults this day," he said. "When my Lord the King was angry with me and put me in prison there was a young man there, a Hebrew, and he was good to me. And one night I dreamed a dream, and he read it for me, and it came true, and my lord the King sent for me that same day. And I have never thought about him from that day to this." But Pharaoh did not mind how the cupbearer had behaved. "Bring him to me at once," he said, and off went the cupbearer and the courtiers running, for Pharaoh's temper was short. Joseph was just starting off with his bunch of keys and his water jug when he heard the thunder at the door. But his heart went no faster. "The King's pardon," he said. "This will be for the head gardener. Poor beggar, he'll be glad to get back to his melons." And he went and opened the door. There stood a crowd of men, and among them one with a face that Joseph thought he knew, only that he was stouter. "That's our man," shouts the cupbearer. "Do you not know me, Joseph? Hurry up, man." And then Joseph knew.

He did not say very much. He only said, very quietly, "You will have to wait till I shave." And he turned and went up to his little room with the barred window, and the keeper of the prison brought him water and sharpened his razor, and stood watching him shave, and telling him how sorry he was that he was going away. And Joseph shaved with a very steady hand, only now and then he felt he wanted to take long breaths. Just as he was going out he stopped and looked round the room where he had lived through such strange white nights of pain. "It is good," he said to himself, "that a man should both hope and quietly wait for the salvation of God."

They had been so quick that Pharaoh was still at table when they brought Joseph in. Joseph might have been nervous if the summons to audience had come when he was still in the house of the Captain of the Guard. But since then he had suffered so much, had come through water so very deep, that he had lost all fear of man. So he bowed himself before Pharaoh, and then straightened himself, and held his peace.

Pharaoh sat and looked at him. "I dreamed a dream last night," he said (for he was a straight-forward person too), "and no one can read it. I have heard that you can read dreams."

"It is not in me," said Joseph. "God shall give Pharaoh an answer of peace."

Pharaoh liked that. Most of the men that he knew bragged of what they could do themselves. So he plunged straight ahead. He was very expansive. He told Joseph that the scraggy cows were so scraggy that he had never seen the like of them in all Egypt for badness. And Joseph listened with steady, understanding eyes. Then when Pharaoh had finished, he spoke. "The dream is from God," he said. "He hath showed Pharaoh what He is going to do. The seven fat cows are seven years of plenty, and the seven lean cows are seven years of hunger, and it will be a great hunger. Men will forget that they were ever anything but hungry, the hunger will be so great. So let Pharaoh do this. Let him look for a man, wise and discreet, and set him over all the land of Egypt. And let men be under him to gather in the fifth part of each harvest, and store it in the King's barns, against the days of hunger, that the people may not die." Pharaoh turned to his councillors. "He has spoken wisely," he said, and they answered, "He has wisely spoken," for the terror of the hunger was upon them. "He has bidden me choose a wise man," said Pharaoh. "Is there any so wise as he with whom is the Spirit of God?" Then he turned to Joseph. "See," said Pharaoh, "I have set thee over all the land of Egypt. Thou shalt be over my house, and over my people. I have given thee all things but my throne, only in that

shall I be greater than thou." He took the ring from his own finger and put it on Joseph's, sent for the robes that only the nobles
wore, and sent him out in his second chariot to make a progress
through the streets, and the people fell on their knees as he went
by. In the evening there was a great banquet. Joseph sat at Pharaoh's right hand, and they drank his health and acclaimed him.
But at last the long day wore to its end, and Joseph went to his
room, lighted on his way by the slaves, the richest room in the
palace after Pharaoh's. But in the doorway he turned and sent
them away, and so went in alone. For a long time he sat very
still.

"It is good," he said, "that a man should both hope and quietly
wait for the salvation of God."

NINE

THERE are eight years between this chapter and the last one. The seven good years were over and done, and the famine had begun, and there were no crops in all the countryside, and the children cried for bread. And then the people began to see why the strange Governor had come round year after year and made them save some of their corn, and had stored it up in great barns in every town. It was there now for the buying, and the fathers went and bought it in sacks, and the mothers ground it and made bread and baked it. And after a while they began to see strange men coming along the roads, riding on camels and on donkeys, hungry-looking men who could speak no Egyptian but the word for corn. They were coming from all the countries outside Egypt, for there was bad harvesting and hunger everywhere, and Egypt was the only place where people had been wise enough to save. These strangers were going on to the City of the Sun, where the biggest barns were, for Joseph said that he would sell to the foreigners himself, and see to it that they were honest men and not spies. For there were spies in those days just as clever as they are now. Joseph was called the Governor of Egypt, and people talked about him as they talked about the King, and told stories about him, and how beautiful his wife was, and how fond he was of his little sons. For Joseph had married one of the noblest of the Egyptian women—her name was Asenath—and they had two sons. And when the first boy was born Joseph was so utterly content that he called him Manasseh, which means Forgetfulness, for he said, "God has made me forget all my toil, and all my father's house."

But this morning Joseph wakened early, early enough to hear the swallows talking to themselves in their nest under the eaves.

And suddenly he seemed to remember the mornings years and years ago when he was little, and lay awake looking up at the black tent over his head, and heard the chirping of the birds in the old oak. And a strange hunger came on him to see it all again —the old black tent, and the smoke of the camp fire, and his father sitting at the door. He remembered Benjamin, too, and how young he looked when you saw his back and his soft neck. Benjamin must have been just about the age of his own small son when Joseph bade him good-bye that morning: and Joseph remembered how he had wanted to go with him, and how he had cried. Of a sudden he felt lonely. It was all very well to be Governor of Egypt and the richest man under the King, to be great and stately and have people bowing down before you when you went through the streets. He wanted his own folk. He wanted somebody to call him "Joseph," not "my lord." His children called him father, and his wife called him by his great Egyptian name. There was not anybody to speak to him in his own tongue. He thought of the big brothers who had sold him, and somehow all the anger at them had gone out of his heart. There was not one of them he would not have been glad to see, and as for Reuben, the big, lazy, kindly one, if he could have seen him lounging across the grass with his slow smile, he would have hugged him. "Good old Reuben," he said to himself and the slave who had been waving the great fan behind his bed dropped it, and prostrated himself, and said, "Did my lord speak?" and Joseph sighed and got up. It was not easy to forget that he was Governor of Egypt.

But all morning the old days kept coming back to him. He sat in the Chamber of Audience, and the slaves came and went, ushering in the foreigners who came with their gold to buy. But every now and then he dropped his head upon his hands and saw it all again—the tent door and the dogs asleep, and Benjamin digging with a pointed stick, and somewhere down the hill Reuben shouting at somebody to hurry up. He could have sworn that it was Reuben's voice, it was so near, and he raised his head, half thinking that his dream had come true. But he was in the Chamber of Audience, on his chair of state, with the lions on the steps, and at the far end of the hall the slaves had swung back the curtains and were ushering in a fresh crowd of buyers. Joseph looked at them wearily as they came slowly up the hall. There were ten of them, he counted, and they looked dusty and fagged and travel-stained, as if they had come from afar. Their heads were bowed, for they were in the presence of the greatest man in Egypt, and his magnificence was a strange thing to them, and made them ill at ease. But as they fell on their faces before him, one of them shot a glance at the man they had come so far to seek, and Joseph met his eyes. It was only a moment, but it seemed to Joseph as if something had snapped in his heart. He rose to his feet and stood looking down at them where they lay before him. These were his brothers, and they did not know him. And the man who held their life in his hands was the boy they had sought to kill.

T E N

For a long time Joseph sat, holding the arms of his chair, and gazing straight before him. There was silence in the place, for no man may speak without leave in the presence of the King, and Joseph was in the King's stead in Egypt. His brothers still knelt bowed before him, and he sat high above them, looking and remembering all things. The interpreter beside him fidgeted a little. He was wondering why his lord's face was so strained and set, and why he kept silence so long. But he had been absent-minded and unlike himself all day. At last the interpreter coughed discreetly behind his hand, and Joseph roused himself.

"Whence come ye?" he said. He spoke in Egyptian and his voice was harsh. His brothers sat back on their knees, and looked at him fearfully. "My lord says 'Whence come ye?'" said the interpreter. It was Judah who spoke. It was always Judah who drove the bargains in the old days, Joseph remembered. Judah was the business man of the family, far more than slack old Reuben.

"From the land of Canaan we are come, to buy food," said Judah. It was the first time Joseph had heard the old Hebrew tongue for more than twenty years, and it went to his heart. But he had his part to play, and he turned a blank face to the interpreter as if he had not known what had been said.

Then for a while he sat and frowned at them. "Ye be ten men," said Joseph. "Why are there ten of you journeying together? Ye are spies—ye are come to see the weakness of the land."

"My lord," said Judah earnestly, "we are ten men journeying together, because we are brothers, and we are come to buy food. We are all sons of one father; we are true men, and not spies."

"Ye are spies," said Joseph, and his voice was level and hard.

[41]

"Ye are spies; to spy out the weakness of the land are ye come."

His brothers looked at one another in dread. "My lord," said Judah desperately, "it is not so. Thy servants are brothers; there are twelve of us altogether, and the youngest of us is this day with our father and one—" he stopped. He was looking into the eyes of the Governor of Egypt, and yet all at once he seemed to see the eyes of the little lost brother who had cried and clung to his knees. Judah groaned. "But one," he said, "is not."

Joseph rose to his feet. "Ye are spies," he said coolly. "If ye are not, prove it. Let one of you go and bring your youngest brother, that I may see if there is any truth in you, and the rest of you shall be kept in prison till he comes. For I swear to you by the life of Pharaoh,"—the interpreter shook in his shoes—"ye shall not go forth hence unless your youngest brother comes."

"Ho there!" he turned to the guard at the door. "Away with these to the King's prison."

He sat in his chair and watched them marched out, and his face was the face of a graven image. "I will try them," he said to himself, "to see if there is any kindness in them, and if they have repented anything of their hardness of heart. But three days will be enough." In the morning of the third day he sent for them to his presence.

"Ye shall not die," he said, "if ye be true men. Let one of you be bound in the house of your prison, and let the rest of you go and carry corn for the hunger that is in your houses. But bring your youngest brother unto me. So shall I know that ye are true men, and ye shall live and not die."

They turned to one another, and to his surprise there was no relief in their faces. Joseph sat watching them with his hand over his eyes. They were talking despairingly, not knowing that he heard them. "It will kill the old man," they said, "if we take the boy from him. God forgive us! it is a judgment on us for what we did to the wee brother. Boys, do you remember his face that day, and how he cried?" Reuben had been sitting with his face in his hands, and now he looked up. "Did I not tell you?" he cried. "Did I not tell you, 'Do not sin against the child?' and you would not hear. It is his blood that is required of us this day."

Joseph got up suddenly from his chair and went quickly out. Another minute and he would have broken down before them. But in a little while he set his face and came back to them, chose Simeon, and had him bound before their eyes. "Now go," he said, "and bring your youngest brother unto me, and I will deliver this brother unto you again." His heart was eager to give some message to the old man, his father, but he dared not do that yet. Only he told the steward to hide the money that they had paid for their corn in the mouth of every sack, and to give them things to eat on the road; and though they did not see him he stood behind the pillars of the doorway and watched them take the road, the road that he had so often travelled in his dreams, through the desert and over the hills to the green fields of home.

ELEVEN

ONCE again Joseph sat in the Hall of Audience, and the strangers came and went. It was months since the day that he saw his brothers coming up the hall, and sometimes he could have thought it was a dream; only that Simeon was still a hostage in the King's prison. "Will they ever come back, I wonder," he said to himself, "and will they bring Benjamin with them? Unless they are kinder than they used to be, my father will hardly trust them with him. It will go hard with the old man. I wonder was I right to make them bring him—if I shouldn't have told them at once who I was, and sent for them all to come. But if they are the same quarrelsome lot they used to be, they'd only be making mischief. I'll have to wait and see how they treat the boy." And then he would let himself go into a dream about little Benjamin, little Benjamin that he hadn't seen for two and twenty years.

There was a stir and commotion at the doorway, and the keeper of the door came in.

"Sir," he said, "here be the men from Syria, the brethren that ye took for spies."

"Is there a little lad with them?" said Joseph. "Nay," said the slave, "but a young man, well-grown and slender."

"Take them to my house," said Joseph, "and bid the steward make ready a feast, for they shall dine with me at noon."

It seemed a long morning to Joseph, watching the strangers come and go, but at last it wore to mid-day, and he was free.

"Did you make the men welcome?" he said to his steward, as he poured water over his hands. "They were sore afraid at first," said the steward, "for they thought you had meant to trap them for the money that was in their sacks, but I bade them be at ease, that God had given them the money, and I brought them water to wash their feet and fodder for the asses." "You have done well," said Joseph, and went into the hall.

They were prostrate on their faces as he came in. He saw the presents that their old father had sent him to soften his heart towards them, balm and honey and spices and myrrh and nuts and almonds, put up so carefully by his old hands, and he could have cried. "Tell me," he said, "is your father well, the old man of whom ye told me? Is he yet alive?" They raised their heads and said, "Thy servant, our father, is yet alive." Joseph was looking them over one by one, and at last he saw a young face, not of the little Benjamin, digging in the sand, but not unlike the face that he used to see reflected in the fishponds when he went to measure the depth. "Is this the youngest brother?" he said softly. "God be gracious unto thee, my son," and with that he turned and went quickly out. The old days were tugging at his heart, and he must not break down before them. But once in his own room he dropped his head in his hands and wept.

It was not for long. Joseph had learned to command himself in Egypt, and he dashed cold water on his face and went back, quiet and impassive. It was a wonderful feast, but more than at all the strange dishes the brothers marvelled at Joseph himself. He had them placed at table as if he knew their ages—Reuben first, and Benjamin last, and he sent them dishes from his own table, though the best share always went to Benjamin. Joseph watched to see if it made them jealous, but they only seemed the better pleased. Joseph watched them laughing and teasing each other, the way brothers who like each other do, and his heart was very soft to them. Now and then they looked up at his table, with the great silver cup shining on it, and above it the Governor's grave, smiling face, and wondered how they had ever feared him.

They were to stay the night. Joseph sat late, but before he went to bed he sent for his steward.

"Let them be asleep," he said, "and then put their money in

their sacks again, and in the sack of the youngest put my great silver cup; and rouse them for the road as soon as it is light." Joseph was waking early, and in the dawn he heard the clinking of hoofs in the yard, and the rattle of harness, and one of his brothers saying with a laugh, "Where's Benjamin? Is he never awake yet, the lazy little cub?" and Judah answering, "Let him have the last minute. I'll saddle for him." "Surely they are changed," thought Joseph, "but I must try them further yet." He lay waking for an hour, and then sent for his steward.

The brothers were beyond the city wall, and trotting along the east road, when they heard a horse galloping behind them. They halted and turned round. It was the steward of the Governor's house, and their hearts sank. He reined up before them and eyed them furiously. "Have ye no grace in you?" he said. "Was it not enough that my lord should feed you at his table, that ye must steal his own drinking cup? This is an evil thing that ye have done."

The brothers gazed at him in bewilderment. Then one spoke out. "God forbid that we should do this thing. Search us and see. And if you find the cup with any of us, he in whose sack it is found shall die, and we his brothers shall be my lord's slaves."

"Good," said the steward, "but we shall not be so hard with you. He with whom it is found shall be the slave; the rest of you shall go your way blameless."

They got down from their asses, and one by one they opened their sacks. Beginning with the eldest, the steward passed from sack to sack till only Benjamin's was left. They opened it, and there gleaming in the corn lay the silver cup.

The steward turned and looked at them. Benjamin was staring at the cup with great bewildered eyes. The others were gazing at each other, dazed.

"I keep to my word," said the steward. "This youngster shall go back with us to answer for it, the rest of you go your ways." The brothers rent their clothes. "We'll die first," they said.

[46]

"Come, let us go together." Joseph, watching, saw the sorry little company clattering back into the yard, Judah—Judah who had sold him—riding beside Benjamin and comforting him.

"Thank God," he said, "I have seen their hearts at last." And so he rose and went down very stately to his judgment seat, and they came before their judge.

TWELVE

JOSEPH looked at them in silence. When he spoke, his voice was indifferent, almost mocking.

"What is this that ye have done?" he said. "Did ye think that I would not find you out?"

It was Judah who answered him, more bravely than he had ever spoken, and more desperately. He had come to the end of all things. "It is God who has found us out," he said, and he was thinking, not of this theft of the cup, but of that old sin against their brother. "Behold, we are thy slaves."

"God forbid," said Joseph. "He with whom the cup was found shall be my slave; the rest of you go in peace to your father."

Then Judah in his agony came a step nearer.

"Oh, my lord, let thy servant, I pray thee, speak a word in my lord's ears, and let not thine anger burn against thy servant; for thou art even as Pharaoh.

"My lord asked his servants, saying, *Have ye a father, or a brother?* and we said unto my lord, *We have a father, an old man, and a child of his old age, a little one; and his brother is dead, and he alone is left of his mother, and his father loveth him.* And thou saidst unto thy servants, *Bring him down unto me that I may set mine eyes upon him.* And we said unto my lord, *The lad cannot leave his father; for if he should leave his father, his father would die.* And thou saidst unto thy servants, *Except your youngest brother come down with you, ye shall see my face no more.*

"And it came to pass when we came up unto my father, we told him the words of my lord. And our father said, *Go again and buy us a little food.* And we said, *We cannot go down; if our youngest brother be with us, then will we go down; for we may not see the man's face, except our youngest brother be with us.*

And my father said unto us, *Ye know that my wife bare me two sons; and the one went out from me, and I said,* 'Surely he is torn in pieces'; *and I saw him not since; and if ye take this also from me, and mischief befall him, ye shall bring down my gray hairs with sorrow to the grave.*

"Now, therefore, when I come to my father, and the lad be not with us; seeing that his life is bound up in the lad's life; it shall come to pass, when he seeth that the lad is not with us, that he will die: and thy servants shall bring down the gray hairs of our father with sorrow to the grave. For thy servant became surety for the lad unto my father, saying, *If I bring him not unto thee, then I shall bear the blame to my father forever.*

"Now therefore, I pray thee, let thy servant abide instead of the lad, a bondman to my lord: and let the lad go up with his brethren. For how shall I go up to my father, and the lad be not with me? Lest peradventure I see the evil that shall come on my father."

Joseph turned to the Egyptians looking on. "Go out from me," he cried, and they went out, wondering, and left him alone with his brethren. Then Joseph turned to them and tried to speak, but instead he broke down, and the loneliness of the years was in his crying, and the house of Pharaoh heard.

At last he spoke—"I am Joseph," he said. "Doth my father yet live?" His brothers stood and looked at him, and could not speak. "Come near to me," said Joseph and held out his hands to them, and they came slowly near. "I am Joseph, your brother," he said, speaking very slowly, that they might take it in, "whom ye sold into Egypt. But you are not to be grieved or angry with yourselves, for God sent me before you to preserve life. For these two years hath the famine been in the land: and there are still five years to come, in which there shall be neither ploughing nor harvest. And God sent me before you to save your lives by a great deliverance. So, now," he almost coaxed them, "it was not you who sent me here, but God; and He has made me a father to Pharaoh, and lord of his house, and ruler of all Egypt. And now, make haste and go to my father and say to him, *'Thy son, Joseph, says: God hath made me lord of all Egypt; come down unto me, and thou shalt dwell in the land of Goshen, and shalt live near me, thou and thy children and grandchildren, and all thy flocks and thy herds, and I will feed thee.'* You see with your own eyes, and my brother Benjamin sees, that it is I who speak to you. And tell my father of all my glory in Egypt, and of all that ye have seen; and ye must haste and bring my father here."

And then he turned and held out his arms to Benjamin, and one by one his brothers came up and he kissed them every one, and after that, it says, they all talked with him.

And so the story goes back to where it began, with an old man sitting at the door of the big black tent, in Hebron, and watching for his sons; and it tells how they came with a great caravan, and how they told the wonderful news, and the old man's heart fainted. He could not believe them. Again and again they told him what Joseph had said, but still he shook his head, and then Judah took his arm and said, "Come and see the fine carriage he sent to bring you to him," and his spirit revived. "It is enough," he said. "Joseph my son, is yet alive; I will go and see him before I die." And the story ends like that other story that our Lord Christ told, "His father saw him, and ran, and fell on his neck and kissed him."

It is a good story to end the year with, for it ends in a reconciling. And when you think of Joseph planning how to bring his brothers' hearts back, will you remember Someone greater than Joseph who devised means that His banished might not be expelled from Him. And when you think of Judah offering to suffer in his little brother's stead, will you remember Someone kinder than Judah who suffered for all His little brothers on the bitter cross. And it is a good story to begin the year with, for, after all, what one sees in it most is not so much the loving kindness of Joseph, as the loving kindness of God, God who redeemeth the souls of His servants.

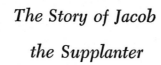

The Story of Jacob

the Supplanter

O N E

I WONDER if you remember how the Joseph story began—an old black tent with a smoke hole in the roof, and an old white-bearded man sitting at the door, leaning on his staff? That was Jacob, the father of all those brothers. This time I want to tell you about him when he was young, as young as any of his sons, and the curious thing is that his story begins just where Joseph's did, in the big black tent. But to begin it properly I shall have to go away back before ever he was born, to the father of Jacob's father, and first of them all to live in the tent under the oak in Hebron.

Long, long ago when Abraham, for that was his name, was a young man, he used to live in one of the richest cities of all the East, in Ur of the Chaldees, the City of the Moon. They called it the City of the Moon because the people in it worshipped the moon-goddess, and had built her a great moon-temple: one can see the ruins of it yet. But one night Abraham was out in the darkness alone, watching the great deep sky and the shining of the stars and the slow rising of the moon. And a hunger came upon him for a God who was not like the moon, far away and different and cold, but a God who was like himself, only greater far. He fell on his face and prayed, not to the sky or the moon or the stars, but to Someone behind them all, and even as he prayed a voice spoke, not far off, but in his very heart. "Abram," it said, "get thee out of thy country and away from thy father's house, to the land that I will show thee; and I will make of thee a great nation, and thou shalt be a blessing to all the earth." And Abraham went out, not knowing whither he went. He crossed the great river, the river Euphrates, journeying by day and pitching his tent by night, on and on till he came to the land of Canaan, and there one night he heard the voice again, saying, "Unto thy sons will I give this land." And Abraham believed God. On and on he went, still journeying to the south, till at last he came to Hebron, to the great oak on the hill, and pitched his tent, and built an altar, and there stayed. All round him the people of the land were worshipping other gods, the moon and the stars and trees and stones, and they wondered at this man who was so stately and so gracious, and who prayed to a God that no one could see. For years he lived among them, but he was always different; and when they talked of him among themselves they called him "the Hebrew"—the man from beyond the river.

But Abraham grew old. One day he lay looking through the tent door at the far hills over which he had come so many years ago, and he was thinking of his dead wife and of Isaac his son. It was three years since she had died and left her tent empty; and they were lonely, the old man and the young man, with no woman to care. Isaac had never got over his mother's death; it would comfort him if he could find a wife like her, and bring her home to his mother's tent. But not the women of that country; they were a bad stock. What if he could find one of the daughters of his own people, away in Mesopotamia beyond the river, some girl like what his mother had been, gracious and fair and young? Abraham sat up and clapped his hands, and his old steward came running. "Swear to me," said Abraham, "that you will never take a wife for my son from the women here, but that you will go away back to my own country and my own kin, and take a wife for him there."

"Master," said the steward, "I will go. But if the girl says she will not come with me to a strange land, what then? Shall I come back for my master Isaac, that he may plead with her himself?"

Abraham lay and thought of the old rich life and the lure of it. If Isaac went would he ever come back to live in tents, a stranger in a strange land? "Swear," he said, "that you will never take Isaac there, but go yourself, and God will send His angel before you."

So the old steward swore. And out he went and chose ten camels, strong and surefooted, and loaded some with dates and figs and wine and bread, and some with rich stuffs, purple and scarlet and cloth of gold for presents to this unknown wife, and on his own camel he fastened a little casket of jewels, gold ear-rings and gold bracelets, smiling to himself, for he thought, "The child will like these, or she is no woman." And so early one morning he said good-bye to Abraham and went his way.

Day after day he travelled, for from Hebron to Haran is four hundred miles. But at last one evening he came to the city of palm trees, and stopped beside the well outside the gate, and made the camels kneel down, for they were very tired. "What city is this, my son?" he said to a small boy driving home a goat. "The city of Nahor," says the small boy, and shouted at the goat to hurry up. The old steward went over to his camels and stood still. He had reached his journey's end, for Nahor was the name of his master's brother, and this was the city of his master's kin. But how of all the girls of the city was he to choose his young master's wife? Standing there by his camels the old steward began to tell God all about it. "O Lord God of my master Abraham," he said, "You see me here beside the well of water, and it is the time in the evening when the young girls come out with their pitchers to draw water; will You let it be this way, that if I say to one of them, 'Let down your pitcher, I pray you, and give me a drink,' and if she answers, 'Drink, and I will bring some water for the camels too,' it will be a sign to me, and I shall know that You have chosen her to be wife to my master Isaac." Even as he spoke a young girl came through the twilight out of the city gate. She had her pitcher on her shoulder, and she swayed as she went, and she was very fair. She did not see the strange man gazing at her; she went down the steps to the dark old well and filled her pitcher and came up again. But this time the old steward ran

[55]

to meet her. "Let me, I pray you, drink a little water out of your pitcher," he said. The young girl looked at him with great soft eyes. "Drink, my lord," she said, and she hurried to lower the pitcher, and held it while he drank, and he blessed her in his heart for her great gentleness. While he drank she was looking over his shoulder at the poor camels, with their drooping heads and dusty feet, and she saw them looking at the water with mournful eyes. So when he had finished she said, "The camels look so thirsty; I will draw water for them too." And she ran and emptied her pitcher into the stone trough, and went up and down the steps carrying water till the trough was full, and one by one the camels came up and drank till they had all had enough, and camels do drink a lot. And the old man stood at their heads and wondered at her, her gentleness and her patience and her beauty, but he waited and held his peace.

T W O

THE last camel was finishing, drinking very slowly because he knew there were none to come after him and hurry him up; and the old steward went over to his own camel and felt for his little bag of jewels, and chose out of them a precious stone on a ring to wear on the forehead, and two heavy bracelets of gold, and came over to where the young girl was standing. "Tell me, I pray you," he said, "whose daughter are you? And is there room in your father's house that we might lodge there?"

"I am a daughter of Bethuel, who was Nahor's son," said Rebekah, "and there will be room and to spare for you and the camels too."

The old man gazed at her, for it seemed too good to be true. She was as fair and as gentle as heart could desire, and with that she was of his master's own kin, born in the very house that Abraham had left, and the daughter of his brother's son. He took her hands and slipped the great bracelets on her arms, and the ring with the jewel over her hair, and then he turned away and bowed his head, and Rebekah heard him praying, "Blessed be God," he said, "Who hath brought me to the house of my master's brethren." Rebekah did not understand: she looked from the bracelets on her arm to the old man worshipping, and then turned like a swallow and fled to tell her people.

Laban her brother was tall and lean and worldly-wise. He was just sitting down to supper and his mother was saying that Rebekah was long at the well to-night, when she came in, her great eyes shining, and the jewel blazing on her forehead. She held out her arms and they saw the great gold bracelets.

"Where did you get those?" says Laban staring.

"It was an old man with camels come from far," said Rebekah, breathless, "out there by the well. He asked me to let him drink, and I drew water for him and his camels, for they were thirsty; and he asked me whose daughter I was, and when I told him he put these things on my hands, and began to bless God for bringing him to the house of his master's brethren. And he asked if he might stay here." Laban and his mother looked at each other. "I wonder," said his mother slowly, "will it be word from your Uncle Abraham? You would have no memory of him, Laban, for he went away and left us all long before you were born. Some notion he had that God was for giving him a country, and nothing would do him but he must go and look for it. Run, Laban, and see."

"Those are fine presents he gave her anyway," says Laban, and out he went and saw the ten camels standing by the well, and the old steward waiting and looking towards the gates. Laban came up, and the old man and the young man bowed low to each other, the way men do in the East.

"Come in, thou blessed of the Lord," said Laban. "Why standest thou without? There is room for the camels, and the house is ready." They came back together, but the steward would not rest until the camels were lightened of their load, and straw given them to lie on, and fodder, and water for his camel drivers to bathe their dusty feet. Then he came in with salutations, and Rebekah's mother received him, and would have him sit down at the feast she and Rebekah had made ready, but still the old man stood.

"I am Abraham's servant," he said, "and the Lord hath blessed my master. He is become a great prince, and he has flocks and herds, camels and oxen, silver and gold, and all this he has given to Isaac, his only son. And my master made me swear that I would not take him a wife from the women of that country, but that I would seek him a wife from his father's house. And I said, 'It may be that she will not come with me'; and he said, 'The Lord shall send His angel before thee.' So I took my journey, and this day I came to the well, and I prayed that the virgin who would draw water for me and my camels might be the wife that the Lord has chosen for my master's son. And even as I spoke in my heart, Rebekah came forth with her pitcher on her shoulder, and did even as I had said, and I blessed God for her. Now then, the thing is before you. Will you deal kindly with my master and give me Rebekah to be wife to his son, or not? That I may turn to the right hand or to the left."

"It is the hand of God," said Laban. "Rebekah is before thee. Take her and go, for the Lord God has spoken."

Once again the old man bowed his head and worshipped. And then he unpacked his bales, purple and scarlet and cloth of gold, jewels of silver and jewels of gold, and gave them to Rebekah and her mother and to Laban, and so they sat down to the feast. But in the morning, for all his long journey, he was the first astir, and meeting Laban he said, "Send me away, I pray you, to my master."

"Draw your breath," said Laban, "and let Rebekah stay with us this ten days at least, and then take her and go thy way."

"Hinder me not," said the old steward. "Since God hath prospered my way, let me return to my master."

"We will call Rebekah," said Laban. "She shall speak for herself."

So they called Rebekah and said, "Will you go with this man?" All night Rebekah had been thinking of the strange thing that had come into her life at sunset. Of the old prince who saw visions that other men did not see, and who believed that God was giving him a country; and of his son, and the rich jewels he had sent her, and the hundreds of miles this man had come to find her, and how he believed God Himself had chosen her, just because she had been gracious to a stranger at the well. And so when they asked her, "Will you go with this man?" she answered simply, "I will go." And that same day they started on their journey, the long four hundred miles.

And so it came that about the time of the falling of the dew, Isaac went out to meditate in the field at eventide. And he lifted up his eyes and saw, and, behold, the camels were coming. And Rebekah lifted up her eyes, and saw him far off, and said to the old steward, "What man is this who is walking in the field to meet us?" And he looked and said, "It is my master Isaac." And Rebekah took a veil and covered her face, and lighted off the camel that she might meet him. And they went home through the fields together, and Isaac brought her into his mother's tent, and she became his wife; and he loved her, and was comforted for the death of his mother.

And this is how the woman who was to be the mother of Jacob came home.

THREE

Isaac and Rebekah were married for twenty years before they had a son. Rebekah was in sore distress about it. You know, in the East they think that the more children you have the happier you are. And when Rebekah was leaving her mother's house with the old steward they had run out and cried blessings after her and prayed that she might be the mother of a great nation. And then too she remembered the strange promise that God had given to the old prince Abraham, that his children and grandchildren would be as many as the sands of the sea; and would be kings of the country he was living in. How was it going to come true, if she and Isaac had no children? At first she was terribly afraid that Isaac might put her away and take a new wife. In India, it used to be that if a woman had been married seven years without having a son, her husband was allowed to bring home a second wife; and in China he could send her away altogether. But mercifully Isaac cared for her too much. He used to comfort her and tell her that his father and mother had been married twice as long before he was born; but all by himself he prayed and entreated for a son. And after twenty years two boys were born.

They were twins, Esau and Jacob. Esau was born first, a big sturdy fellow, and they called him Redhead, because of his shock of red hair. Jacob they called the Supplanter, because when he was a baby he caught hold of his brother's heel in his tiny fist as if he wanted to haul him back. It was only a jest, yet Rebekah had been praying about them the night they were born, and God told her that each of her sons would be the head of a great nation, but that the elder would serve the younger. It puzzled her. You know even amongst us it is usually the eldest son who gets the business when his father dies, and the younger ones go out from the house and look out for themselves. In the fairy tales it is always the youngest son who goes out to seek his fortune. But in those days in Palestine it meant even more, for the eldest son was the head of the tribe, and could order the others about, like the general of a regiment. It is what is called the Birthright. And it puzzled her even more when the boys were growing up, for the elder one, Esau, was a great big fellow, very strong and very ready with his fists, and always chasing something. And Jacob was a quiet little boy, who liked wandering round by himself in a sort of dream. Esau bullied him a good deal, for he was far the stronger, and used to jeer at him for mooning about, and call him Sleepy Head. And one day their mother caught him punching Jacob's head, and said, "Big and all as you are, it is your little brother will have the Birthright yet." And Esau said, "I don't care. It's all foolish talk about the Birthright anyway. Don't care who gets it as long as I get my fill." And off he went whistling. But Jacob stood looking at his mother.

"What was that you said about my having the Birthright?" he asked her.

His mother stopped. He was staring at her with his eyes very big and very bright.

"I shouldn't have said it," she thought. "You run away and play, there's a good boy."

But Jacob wouldn't run away. "If you don't tell me," he said, "I'll go and ask my father."

His mother weakened. "Well," she said, "it was a dream I had before you were born. I dreamt that God said you would each be the head of a great nation, but that the elder would be servant to the younger. Now just put it out of your head, and run away and play, and don't say a word to your father. Away now."

Jacob did not say a word to anybody. But he did not put it out of his head. He dreamed more and more. He knew all the old stories by heart, how his grandfather had left the City of the Moon to find a country, and how God had promised him this country for his sons and his sons' sons. But what good would that be to Jacob, when Esau had the Birthright? It would all go to Esau. He knew his mother would give it to him if she could, but his father was much fonder of Esau than of him. Esau was always bringing him home venison that he had shot, and then the two had great feasts together. That was all Esau cared about it, tearing about all day, and stuffing himself at night. He wasn't fit to be a King. He hadn't any brains. Jacob despised Esau, just as clever, delicate people despise strong stupid ones, and Esau despised Jacob, just the other way. And so they grew to be men.

One day they went off together, to see after a faraway herd. They had a tent all to themselves, to sleep in at night, and had to do their own cooking, and for a while it was great fun. But one morning Esau got up and said, "You may do what you like, but I'm off for a hunt." He was in such a hurry he didn't wait even to stick a bunch of dried figs in his pocket, and that was the last Jacob saw of him that day. He slept all by himself in the tent, and waited all the next day, until evening came, and still no word. "Must be good hunting," thought Jacob. "I hope he'll bring something home." Jacob hadn't much in the tent, but he put on the pot and was sitting stirring red lentil stew for himself when he saw Esau come trailing over the hill. He was starving: he had shot nothing, hadn't had a bite since he left. Jacob sat still and watched him. He was so faint that he dropped beside the fire.

"Feed me," he said, "with that red—with that red there." He could hardly speak.

Then Jacob did a cruel thing. He stood looking down at the big fellow lying there on the ground.

Who was the stronger now?

"Sell me this day thy Birthright," he said, with a curious light on his face. He had found the way.

"What do I care about it," said Esau, "and me half dead with hunger. Take it and welcome."

"Swear," said Jacob. And Esau swore.

Then Jacob sat down beside him and fed him, gave him stew and soaked bread in it and gave him a drink. And Esau ate his fill, and got up and went whistling out, and never thought about it more. And Jacob thought how well he had managed it. He had got the Birthright that Esau despised. But he had got it by a trick. And God gave him no good of it until He had punished the trickery out of him.

FOUR

I HAVE told you one of the two meanest things that Jacob ever did. This time I have to tell you the other, but after this he begins to be a little nicer.

Esau and Jacob were both of them grown up. Esau had married two wives, heathen girls from round the country; and they quarrelled with each other and quarrelled with Rebekah, and made things so very unpleasant that Esau spent most of his time out hunting. Isaac was an old man now, and spent most of his days lying on his couch at the tent door. He was almost blind, and could hardly see the sunlight, but he liked to feel the fresh air on his face. And in the evenings Esau would come back from the hunt and cook his father some of his venison for supper, and sit beside him while he ate it, and tell all about the long run it had given him, and all the jokes. It was no wonder that his father grew fonder of him every day. Jacob was kind enough, but then he was always about home, and when Esau did come in he had new things to say. Rebekah saw very well how things were going; she knew that Isaac would give all he could to the son he liked best; and she used to sit wondering how she could make what God had said come true—that the elder brother should serve the younger. It never came into her head that if God really meant Jacob to be the chief, He would see to that Himself. As for Jacob, he was content enough. His father might do what he liked, but Esau had sold his Birthright. He used to watch Esau swinging off in the early morning, and wonder if he had forgotten all about it, or if he didn't care. It seemed to Jacob that he gave no more thought to it than if he were one of the beasts that he hunted.

Then came a day that Isaac lay just inside his tent door thinking. Someone went quickly by outside, and Isaac knew the footstep and called, "My son." Esau stopped and said, "What is it, sir?" Isaac lay for a while without speaking. "I am old, Esau," he began at last, "and I know not the day of my death. I want you to take your bow and arrows, and go out and kill me some venison and cook it for me yourself. And so I will give you my blessing before I die."

"All right, sir," said Esau, "but you aren't going to die yet." And away he went. He passed Jacob on the way and chuckled to himself. "He can't take this from me anyway," he thought. "Much good may the Birthright do him, when I have the eldest son's blessing."

But Rebekah, away at the back of the tent, had heard. She lifted the flap of the tent very softly, and stole out to look for Jacob. Jacob was shading his eyes with his hand and looking after his brother, wondering what made him so jaunty, when he heard his mother behind him, and turned round. He knew by her face that something had happened, but he listened quietly till she had told him all. So his big ox of a brother was going to win in spite of all his brains. He sat still, scowling to himself, but his mother was talking on. "Now my son," she said, "you do what your mother tells you. Go down to where the goats are, and choose me two fine kids, and I'll cook them so that your father will never know the difference between them and Esau's venison, and you shall take it in to him and pretend to be Esau, and get the blessing."

Jacob shook his head, not because it was a mean trick, but because he would be found out. "It's no good, mother," he said, "you know what Esau's hands are like, all hairy, and mine are smooth. If my father felt them, he'd know I was tricking him, and it's a curse I'd get and no blessing."

"The curse be on me, my son," said his mother. "You do as I tell you."

Jacob went down to get the kids. He would not let himself think. Something was telling him that it was not fair, that he was being a sneak, but he crushed it down. Esau wasn't fit to get the eldest son's blessing, a great bull like that, with nothing in his head but eating and drinking. His father was too old to know what he was doing; if he had been in his right mind he would have given his blessing to the son that God had chosen to be the chief. Esau had got round him with his venison and his jokes. Jacob came back with the kids, and his mother had been getting out Esau's best clothes, and made him put them on while she roasted the kids. Then she put the skins like gloves on his hands, and sent him in to his father with the savoury meat and the bread. He spoke to his father as he came in, and Isaac said, "Who is it?"

Jacob braced himself for the lie. "I am Esau thy first-born son," he said. "I have done as you told me. Sit up, father, and eat my venison, and then you will bless me."

Now, Esau was often hunting all day before he could find venison, and his father looked puzzled. "How have you been so quick to-day, my son?" he asked.

Jacob had not expected that question. "Because the Lord thy God brought it to me," he said. It was an uglier lie than the first one, for it brought God into it, and that is the meanest lie of all.

Isaac looked still more puzzled. It was not like Esau to say things like that, and the voice sounded different. "Come near, my son," he said. "I want to feel if you are my very son Esau."

So Jacob went near, and his father passed his old hands over the skins. "They are Esau's hands," he said to himself, "but it is Jacob's voice." He sat up, gazing wistfully at Jacob with his sightless eyes.

"Art thou my very son Esau?" he asked, and Jacob said, "I am." He had never felt such a scoundrel in all his life.

So Isaac was content, and ate and drank, and Jacob waited on him. At last his father had done, and the old man said, "Come near and kiss me, my son." And Jacob went near, and his father smelt the open-air country smell that was about Esau's clothes, and held out his hands over his son's head. He blessed him with the dew of heaven and the richness of the earth. "Let people serve thee, and nations bow down to thee; be lord over thy brethren, and let thy mother's sons bow down to thee; cursed be every one that curseth thee, and blessed be every one that blesseth thee." Then he lay back spent and tired, and Jacob helped to put him down, and took the dishes and went away. He had got what he wanted, and he had never felt so poor.

FIVE

THE camp was very quiet as Jacob came out. He stood for a moment at the door of his father's tent, glad to get the air. Not for a good deal would he go through that last half-hour again. It was drawing towards sunset: the shadows of the tents were stretching longer on the dry grass. Jacob looked down the hill to where Esau had pitched his tent, far away from the rest of the camp, and saw the smoke curling up and thought to himself that Esau's quarrelsome wives would be getting his supper ready. Then someone came to the tent door and stepped out, with a smoking dish in his hand, and Jacob dodged round his father's tent out of sight. It was Esau. Jacob had been hot, but the thought of how nearly Esau had caught him tricked out in his clothes turned him cold. He daren't move until Esau would be safe inside. Jacob lay flat on the grass in the shadow at the back of the tent, and smelt the bitter smell of the dust, and watched a grasshopper rubbing his legs, and listened hard.

He heard the footsteps coming up the hill. Esau was a big man, but he stepped lightly as all good hunters do. Isaac had fallen into a doze after his dinner, and did not hear his son coming in. "Now, father," said Esau's big, cheerful voice booming through the tent, "sit up and eat your son's venison, and then you'll give me your blessing." No wonder, Jacob thought to himself, that his father had been puzzled by the difference in the voices. He heard the sound of someone sitting up, and he could see the old man straining his blind eyes to understand.

"Who is it?" said Isaac, bewildered.

"It's your son, father," said Esau, reassuring him. "It's your first-born—Esau."

The old man fell a-shaking. "Who was it," he said, "who came

in here with venison before you, and I ate of it, and blessed him?"
And then the hopelessness of what he had done broke on him.
"Yea," he cried desperately, "and he shall be blessed."

Jacob listening outside raised his head with a sort of fierce joy.
At least they could not take that from him. Then a great cry came
from inside the tent, so great and bitter that he shuddered at it.
Esau had fallen on his knees.

"Bless me, even me also, O my father!" he pleaded, holding out
his hands: but Isaac looked hopelessly past him.

"Thy brother came with subtlety," he said, "and took away thy
blessing."

"Jacob?" said Esau, and he spoke as if it were a snake. "Jacob—
the Supplanter. They did well to call him that. Twice has he done
it. He took away the Birthright, and now he has taken away the
blessing. O my father," the cry came into his voice again, "hast
thou kept no blessing for me?"

Isaac was shaking with his distress. "Behold," he said, "I have
made him thy lord, and I have given him his brethren for servants.
And I have blessed him with corn and wine. O my son, what shall
I do for thee?"

"Hast thou only one blessing, O my father?" said Esau. "Bless
me, even me also, O my father," and with that he fell to sobbing,
and Jacob—outside—buried his face in his hands that he might not
hear.

Then Isaac began to speak, and Esau hushed his crying. And
Isaac blessed him with the blessings of the open field and the
blessings of the dew. "Thou shalt serve thy brother," he said, "but
it shall be by the sword. And the day will come when thou shalt
break his yoke from off thy neck."

There fell a silence. Isaac's hand fell from Esau's bowed head,
and he lay back, tired out. There was the sound of someone rising
heavily to his feet, and Jacob did not wait for more. Once Esau
was free of his father's tent, he would go through the camp like
a wild bull, looking for his brother. Jacob plunged for a little dry

water-course that ran down the hill, and fled down it, keeping his head low. There was a tiny cave at the foot of the hill that had been his secret place when he was a little fellow and Esau was bullying him—and Jacob made for it now. There is always the chance of a snake in a place like that, and he stopped to rattle a stick through it, but nothing came out, and he stooped his head and crept in. His old friend the toad was sitting in one corner of it, but he did not croak or move. Jacob lay down with his chin on his hands, and waited for the dark. The sun set very far off. Then the dew fell, and the dust smelt the bitterer for it, and the toad came and sat at the mouth of the cave. Jacob spoke to him and scratched his back, but the toad took no notice of him. Then the stars rushed out—the stars that Jacob had always thought so much kinder than the moon—but they took no notice of him either. He lay still, staring at the white, dry dust between his elbows. Nothing had anything to say to him. He had not even anything to say to himself.

SIX

IT WAS a long time before Jacob stirred. Up on the hill he could hear the faint evening noises of the camp, the rattle of the oxen being unyoked, and the lowing as they went down to the water in the valley. It was strange to be out of it all. It was like when you have been sent to bed in the daytime, and you hear the clinking of the cups being laid for tea, and you feel very far off.

But at last the camp fell quiet, and the wind brought only the smell of the smoke from the dying fires, and Jacob crawled out and stretched himself and went up the hill. He stepped carefully, even though the tents were dark, and everyone seemed asleep. In his mother's tent a light was still burning. He hesitated as he went by, and his mother's voice said softly, "Is that you?" He lifted the flap and went in.

His mother sat back on her heels and looked at him. She was packing a bundle. Jacob could see all his clothes scattered round her. "Your brother has sworn to kill you," she whispered. "You will have to go." Jacob said nothing. His mother came nearer, coaxing him. "It will only be for a little while," she said. "I am going to send you to my brother in Haran. You know what Esau is like— soon angry and soon cooled. It will only be a few days till I send for you."

She went on talking, but Jacob did not hear. He was only seeing one thing: that he was to go; leave the camp and the old ways that he had lived and cheated and lied for, and go among strangers. This was what his scheming had come to, that he must sneak out of the camp like a thief. He stood still, staring straight before him. "O my son," his mother's voice broke into a cry, "why should I lose you both in one day?" Jacob roused himself. "I will go," he said dully, and went out.

All the next day Jacob went about like a man dazed. There was no fear of Esau, for early in the morning he was up and away on a gazelle-hunt, to get rid of his anger in the south country. Jacob went to say good-bye to his father, and heard the old stately blessing pronounced over his head, but the words went past him. Then he kissed his mother and took his stick and went. He supposed it would hurt him to-morrow, but to-day he was too numb to care. Only at the turn of the road, where one saw the trees for the last time, he stopped and looked back, and then went on with his eyes fixed on the dusty road. He did not see them again for thirty years.

Most of the night he travelled, and all the next day except when the sun was hottest, and he lay under a sycamore and slept a little. He met shepherds on the hills here and there who knew him, and stopped him to ask for his father, and he answered them civilly and tramped on. But the second day he was in a strange country, and a wilder. And towards evening the road began to climb up into the mountains. Jacob hurried, for it was a desolate place to be alone in, and once the sun set the darkness would come quickly. He looked about him as he went for some shepherd's tent to spend the night in, but there seemed to be no one but himself on the hills. The road dipped into a rocky little valley, and just as he reached it the sun went down. Jacob stood still and looked about him for a glimmer of fire, for fire shines far at night, but there was nothing but the great shoulders of the hills and the quiet sky. He dared go no further for he might lose his way, and be wandering there for days. So he chose out a comfortable big boulder to lie down beside, and a stone to put under his head, and lay down with his arms flung across his face to shut out the unfriendly stars. He did not say his prayers. What was the use? He had left God away behind him, watching over the old camp. There was no one to care for him in all the world.

And then, in the middle of the night, the vision came. He dreamed, and in his dream he saw great stairs rising at his feet and climbing up till they reached the sky. And on them angels passed each other going up and down, and at the top there was a great shining that lightened all the hills. And a voice spoke to him out of the glory of light, and suddenly it crashed upon Jacob's soul that God was speaking to him, just as He had spoken to the old prince Abraham and his father. At first it was the promise that he knew by heart, of the country for an inheritance, but then the voice changed and began saying things that were for Jacob alone. "I am with thee," it said, "and will keep thee in all places whither thou goest, and bring thee again into this land: for I will not leave thee until I have done that which I have spoken to thee of." Then the vision passed, and Jacob awoke with a great fear upon him.

"Surely the Lord is in this place," he said, "and I knew it not. This is none other than the house of God and this is the gate of heaven."

At last the dawn broke, and daylight came flooding over the hills. Jacob rose to his feet, still shaken, but steadier. He took the stone that had been his pillow and set it up and poured oil on it to make it sacred; and then he stood looking up into the blue, empty sky. He was not sure that God was there, but he thought that He might hear him anyway. "If God will be with me," he began soberly, going step by step over what he had heard last night, "and if He will keep me in the way that I go, and will give me bread to eat and raiment to put on" (he thought he had better put that in), "so that I come again to my father's house in peace, then shall He be my God, and this stone that I have set for a pillar shall be God's house and—" of a sudden Jacob realised that God was listening, and he spoke to Him straight—"of all that Thou shalt give me I will surely give the tenth unto Thee." He stood a little while, then he picked up his stick and went his way.

Now there were two mistakes that Jacob made, and it was little wonder if he did, for we make them ourselves every day. He thought that that little rocky valley was the only place that was the Gate of Heaven, and that he had stumbled on it by accident:

and what God wanted him to see was that the great stairway was beside him all the time, and that all day long the angels go up and down it between Him and us, like the great shafts of light that we only see at sunset. And the other mistake was that he offered God his things, and not himself. *God did not want Jacob's tithes: he wanted Jacob.* But it was twenty years before Jacob found that out.

But there was a bigger mistake that he might have made, and he did not. It would have been easy for Jacob when the morning came, with the sunlight filling the valley and the blue sky with white clouds sailing where the top of the stairway had been, to think that it was not real, that he had made it up in his sleep. But he did not do that. He knew that he was not good: he knew that he was not fit to meet God: but he knew that he *had* met Him. He had found out one of the strangest things that anyone can ever find out—that the most real things in the world are the things that you do not see.

SEVEN

I WANT you to get a map and look for Mesopotamia, the place where Jacob was going. Mesopotamia is called by the Arabs "the island," because two big rivers run round it, rivers with splendid names, the Tigris and the Euphrates. Some of the most sounding names in the world are here. There is Babylon, which is like a temple gong, and Nineveh, and Ur of the Chaldees; and the river Ulai, which is surely a wonderful name for flowing water, and further away Mount Orontes and Ecbatana, and the city of Baghdad.

Even in Jacob's time, these cities—all but Baghdad—were old. But round about Haran there were only great stretches of quiet land, and here and there a little village with a wall round it and a well outside the gate. Somewhere in his journeying Jacob crossed the Euphrates, the great river that his grandfather Abraham had crossed long before him, going the other way. You remember how the people in Palestine called him "the Man from Beyond the River." After that Jacob knew he had not far to go, for when he was little he used to get his mother to draw him a picture in the sand of all the way she had come, riding on a camel, to be married to his father, and the big river was always near the beginning. And so one hot afternoon he came in sight of palm trees, and a little walled town, and three great flocks of sheep waiting outside the gate. Three herdsmen were sitting, cross-legged, under the trees at the well, half asleep in the heat. They looked at Jacob when he came up, but they did not stir.

"My brethren," said Jacob politely, "where do you come from?"

They raised their heads and said, "Of Haran are we," and settled down again. They did not ask Jacob where he came from, because they were sleepy, and it was very hot.

Jacob stood looking at them. "Haran"; then he had reached his journey's end. "I wonder," he said to himself, "would they know my uncle?" He coughed apologetically, but they took no notice, so he plunged. "Know ye Laban, the son of Nahor?" he asked.

They looked up wearily. "We know him," they said patiently, and again their chins sank on their breasts.

Jacob wriggled. "Is he well?" he ventured.

By this time they felt there was no quieting him. "He is well," they said. "And behold," added one of them with a sudden gleam, "there is his daughter Rachel coming with the sheep." Jacob turned and looked with the curious feeling that it had all happened already, long ago. It was like the old story, he thought: here was a young girl coming to the well, just as his mother had come long before he was born; and here was himself, come all those leagues to meet her. Was it to meet her? Was this the woman who was to be his wife?

She had come nearer. He could see how young she was, and how slender. Jacob turned to the herdsmen who had lapsed again, and were very nearly sound asleep. The well was covered with a huge stone to keep the dust out of it. Was that slip of a girl to wait till these lazy hulks had all their sheep watered? "Why don't you water the sheep?" he asked a little impatiently. "The sun is high yet, and it is hours till folding-time. Water them and take them to pasture."

They opened their eyes and looked at him mildly. "We wait," they said placidly, "till all the sheep are here, and till someone rolls away the stone. It is a heavy stone."

Jacob turned his back on them, and stooped over it. It was a heavy stone, but he set his teeth and tugged. They watched him amiably and thought that he was an energetic young man, but they did not offer to help. At last the stone went back with a great heave, and Jacob straightened himself with a swing of his shoulders, and turned to find Rachel gazing at him. Then Jacob did the suddenest thing he had ever done in his life; he stooped and kissed her. And then he did what surprised himself even more—he cried.

He was too big to cry, of course. But he had been tramping for weeks without seeing a face he knew, and he was sick with loneliness. He pulled himself together in a minute, and told Rachel who he was, and she made much of him, very shyly, for her heart was soft towards him. They began watering the sheep together, and then Rachel left him to finish and ran home to tell her father, and old Laban came out to meet him, and made a great fuss of him, and brought him home.

They sat long over the supper. It was a fine supper, for while Jacob was helping Laban to fold the sheep, Leah and Rachel were cooking for him, roasting him a kid, and baking him fresh hot bread, and getting out honey and fresh figs and grapes. Leah was Rachel's elder sister, not so lovely, and because of it a little wistful, with great soft eyes. They surprised Jacob afresh every time he looked at her, but that was not very often for Rachel sat beside her. Laban talked and talked; asked how his mother kept her health, and how many head of cattle his father had, and if it was hard to get help at the sheep-shearing, and how long the rains lasted. And Jacob sat trying to attend to his uncle's questions, and wondering when Rachel would lift her head and look at him. Jacob had thought he was hungry, but he was too much excited to eat. He had thought he was tired out, but when he went to bed he was too eager to sleep. His mind would do nothing but go over and over all the few things she had said to him, and how she had looked when she said them. For the first time in his life Jacob had found that it was possible to care for someone else more than for himself. And so, for the second time, he was found by the grace of God.

EIGHT

FOR a month Jacob lived with Laban his uncle. That first night he told Laban all that had come upon him, and how it was that he came like a tramp from his father's house. And Laban said, "Thou art my bone and my flesh," and made him as welcome as if he had come with a train of camels. For though Laban was a mean man, his law was the law of the East: to turn no stranger from your door; never to forget your kin. But Jacob would not eat his bread in idleness. Every morning he went out with the sheep to pasture, and watched them through the burning heat of the day; and in the cool of the evening he brought them to the well beside the gate, and sometimes Rachel was at the well, and they watered the flock together. It was always Rachel, for Leah would be getting supper ready in the house. And even at supper she was too busy serving to do more than look at Jacob with her wistful eyes. For Jacob loved Rachel, but Leah loved Jacob.

Now Jacob was wise with the sheep. He never drove them hard, or hurried them, as Rachel sometimes did; and he never let them drink when they were very hot. Laban saw that they were thriving well with him, and he saw too that the boy was getting restless, and wondered what he could do to keep him. Jacob *was* restless, but it was not, as his uncle thought, because he wanted to better himself. It was because he wanted Rachel; and how was a wanderer like himself to ask her of her father in marriage? They sat at the tent door together one night in the starlight, Jacob mending the thong of his sandal, and straining to hear what Rachel was saying to Leah (they were grinding corn together at the back of the tent), Laban, stroking his long, white beard, and pondering. "I cannot think to keep him always for nothing but his bread and salt," he thought to himself. "I will speak to him of wages, and let him name his own, for he will ask less of me than I could offer him." He cleared his throat, and Jacob looked up.

"You are my brother, and the son of my sister," the old man began (to say "my brother" is the Arab way of speaking of your kin); "but because you are my brother should you serve me for nought? Tell me, what shall your wages be?"

A great light leaped into Jacob's eyes. He was an outcast from his own people, but he knew the worth of his hands, and he knew that he could claim high wages from many masters, for it was a great country for sheep. And he knew that Laban was mean, and that it came hardly to him to give money down. But the thing that he was going to ask was to him a thing so precious that he feared lest he should offer too little.

"I will serve thee seven years," he said slowly, "for Rachel thy younger daughter."

Laban started. He had thought he must give a great dowry with his daughter in marriage, and here was this man asking for no dowry; selling himself for seven years for a slip of a girl at the end of it. Inwardly Laban blessed him for a fool, but outwardly he looked on him benignly.

"It is better that I give her to you," he said, "than that I should give her to another man. Abide with me." So they crossed hands solemnly upon it, and Laban rose up and went contentedly to bed. But Jacob went out under the stars, for his happiness was too wild for sleep. He had done a mad thing; he had sold himself for seven years, made himself a slave with not so much as would buy him fresh sandals when these wore out; but it was the wisest and the greatest thing he had ever done. All his life Jacob had taken all he could and given not at all. Now for the first time he gave and gave greatly; himself, for seven years of his youth.

He wandered under the stars on those same plains where Satan had said to God, sneering, "Skin for skin, yea, all that a man hath will he give for his life." But Jacob's heart was crying, "Life for life, yea, all that a man hath will he give for his love."

And the marvel of it is, that the glory of it never went from him. He had time enough to repent of it in the seven years that came after, seven years of watching and wandering, short nights under the summer stars, longer nights in the bitter frosts, nights when the lions were out, and he sat waking from dark till dawn, not daring to let the watchfire die, lonely months when he changed the pasture, slow-moving with the sheep, and did not so much as see her face. "Jacob served seven years for Rachel," the story says, "and they seemed unto him but a few days for the love he had to her." That verse is a great lyric; and because of it Jacob the Supplanter is among the great lovers of the world.

None the less, he kept his count. And when the day came that he had struck hands with Laban seven years before, Jacob came to him and said, "Give me my wife, for I have served my time." And Laban gathered together all the men of the countryside, and made them a great feast that lasted all the day. And when the evening came, and they were beyond themselves with feasting and shouting and laughter, Laban brought in the bride to her husband, veiled, for that was the custom of the East, so that no man saw her face, and the two were made man and wife. And then for the first time Jacob saw her—and it was Leah!

He went out, blind in his anger. "What is this that you have done to me?" he asked Laban. "Did I not serve with you for Rachel? Wherefore then have you cheated me?"

"Peace, young man," said Laban soothingly. "Leah is the elder. It is not so done in our country, to give the younger before the first-born. Let the marriage week be ended, and we will give you this girl also"—he hesitated and looked sideways at the wrathful face confronting him—"for the service which you shall serve with me yet another seven years."

Jacob turned his back on the old man and stood gazing over

the plains to the blue hills of home. Seven more years before he could take his wife and go back to his father's house! Seven more years, and be empty at the end of them as when he came. *Life for life, yea, all that a man hath will he give for his love.*

"I will do it," he said, and went back to where Leah awaited him with beautiful miserable eyes. She had deceived him, and her father had deceived him: they had come with subtlety. And then a cold wind blew over Jacob's heart. Just seven years ago he had heard Esau's voice in that bitter cry, and his father's sentence on him: "Thy brother came with subtlety and hath taken away thy blessing." As he had done to others, so was it done to him.

NINE

LABAN sat at his tent door in the evening, with his legs crossed and his hands folded, and listened to the bleating of his sheep.

Laban was very well content. Fourteen years, he counted, since young Jacob had come to him and he had taken him in; the best day's work he ever did in his life. Jacob had brought luck with him. Then he counted his sheep by scores; now he could count by hundreds. He had never had a herder like him: and honest, too, for if ever he lost a sheep or the wild beasts tore it, Jacob paid for it.

And in return for it all, he had been fool enough to ask only for a wife. Laban smiled to himself remembering the wrathful face of him the morning that he tricked him about Leah. But he had got another seven years' work out of him by it, and after all two wives were better than one. It was a pity they quarrelled so much. But Leah's sons were fine boys, and Rachel would be happier and not so jealous now that she had a son of her own. A fine baby he was too, and Jacob seemed fonder of him already than of Leah's six. That would be because he liked Rachel better even yet.

Laban thought one woman was as good as another, but Jacob always was a fool in some things. Then Laban roused himself, for he saw a figure coming through the dark from the cluster of lights that were Jacob's tents, and he knew by the long stride that it was Jacob.

"It is a fine evening," said Laban politely.

"It is fine," said Jacob; but his voice did not sound as if he were thinking of what he said. Laban sat up to make room for him on his sheepskin, but Jacob stood. He was gazing, not at

Laban, but at the far blue line where the mountains of Gilead heaved their shoulders against the stars.

Laban wondered a little at the look on his face. To be a good business man, Jacob had a way of looking as if he were dreaming on his feet. He coughed a little. Jacob stirred, and looked down at the old man sitting before him. Then he began to speak, with a strain in his voice.

"Send me away," he said. "I want to go to mine own place."

Laban stared. Wasn't one place as good as another?

"I want to go to mine own place," said Jacob, and he turned again to the hills, "and to my country. Give me my wives and my children, and let me go. You know how I have served you."

Laban was thinking rapidly. He could not let Jacob go. He would bribe him with high wages.

"If you care for me at all, Jacob," he said wistfully, "stay with me a little. Ever since you came into this house the Lord has blessed me; I have learned that. Stay, and you may name your own wages."

Jacob turned on him. "I have served you," he said, "you know that. For a little flock you have a multitude. When am I going to provide for mine own house?"

"What shall I give you?" asked Laban meekly. In his heart he knew the boy was right. He had given fourteen years, and had as little now as when he came.

"I am not asking you to give me anything," said Jacob proudly. "But let me take the brown sheep—you know there are not many—and the speckled cows, and the speckled goats. Let me have these for my own, and I will serve you a while longer."

"Just as you say, my son," said Laban. "We'll divide the herds to-morrow." So Jacob said good-night and went back to his tent, passing the tent where Rachel lay asleep with her first-born baby beside her.

After all, it was better to stay. He could not go home a beggar, with all these to provide for. It would only be a few more years.

Meantime Laban was rousing his sons. "Boys," he said, "Jacob is for leaving us, as soon as he gets his share of the brown sheep and the speckled cattle. Up and choose them out, and away with you and them to the back of the desert, or it is leaving us he will be to-morrow."

Up they got, grumbling and sleepy. In the morning Laban and Jacob went through the herds: there was hardly a speckled coat among them. Laban was half afraid of a blaze of anger, but Jacob set his mouth and said nothing. And Laban did not make much of his trickery, for when the next lambing time came, the best of the new lambs and kids were brown and speckled.

So it was every year, until Laban grew angry, and so did his sons. For Jacob had grown rich: he had sheep and cattle, and menservants and maidservants, and camels and asses. He was living like a prince, they said, and all this glory at their father's expense. Jacob saw the change in their faces, and every day his heart grew sick for home.

And then, one night, he had a vision. Once again the glory shone about him, and a voice said, "Jacob"—the same voice that he had heard in the hollow of the hills at Bethel twenty years ago. And Jacob said, "Here am I."

"I have seen all that Laban doeth unto thee," the voice went on. "I am the God of Bethel, where thou didst anoint a pillar, and vow to me a vow. Arise, get thee out from this land, and return unto the land of thy fathers: and I will be with thee."

In the morning Jacob sent for his wives to the field, and told them, and they bade him go. "Our father counts us strangers," they said. "Take us and our children, and whatever God has said, that do."

It so happened that Laban had gone to the sheep-shearing. Jacob rose up, and set his wives and his children on camels, and divided the cattle and sheep in droves, and set off across the plains.

Once again he crossed the great river, that he had forded alone twenty years ago. Now it took hours to cross, for the cattle were afraid of the water, and there was great running and shouting and splashing. But at last they were all safely over, and Jacob set his face to the mountains, and journeyed on.

Day after day they journeyed, looking back now and then to see if they were pursued, till at the end of the seventh day they reached the mount of Gilead, and pitched their tents for the night. And as he stood giving orders, Jacob shaded his eyes with his hand and saw far off a cloud of dust, and in it sparks of glittering light, and knew it for spearpoints flashing in the sunset.

He stood and watched them coming, but he was not afraid. "I have clean hands," he said to himself, "and a good quarrel. And God is on my side." They came nearer; he saw them picketing their horses across the valley, and their camp fires twinkling out one by one. "They will not attack to-night," said Jacob, and he went to his tent.

TEN

IT WAS a long night. Jacob lay looking through the door of his tent, watching the camp fires twinkling across the valley. Men passed backwards and forwards from the tents, and he saw the sparkle of spearheads red in the fire-light. All Laban's sons were there, desert riders all of them, and armed. What was he with his handful of young sons and a few frightened herdsmen, against them? What would happen to-morrow? Would they take his wives and his children and the herds, and go riding back to their own place, and leave him to crawl back to his father's house, lonely and beggared as when he came out? Or would they kill him? At last the dawn broke. Haggard and desperate, Jacob got up and went down to the valley, with the heart in him dead.

They saw him coming from where they sat over the camp fire. The brothers rose to their feet, reaching for the spears that lay beside them, and stood in a cluster scowling, while one ran to the centre tent to rouse their father. Then the white-headed old man came out, and looked, and Jacob stopped, watching for him to give the word. He lifted his hand and spoke, but instead of an answering yell and a flight of spears, they stood staring at their father, and one by one they slowly dropped their arms. Laban himself came down the hill. It was Jacob's turn to stand and stare, for when the old man came near enough, he saw in his face not anger, but a strange kind of awe.

"You did foolishly, my son," said Laban in his mild old voice. "Why did you steal away from me and carry off my daughters, as if they were captives taken with the sword? Why did you not tell me, if you sore longed after your father's house, that I might have sent you away with mirth and songs and tabret and harp? Why did you not suffer me to kiss my sons and my daughters?"

Jacob had not spoken. If this was all Laban had to say, need he have come seven days' hard riding over the desert, with a train of armed men, to say it? Laban saw the doubt on his face.

"It is in the power of my hand to do you hurt," he went on a little proudly. "But," and the look of awe came back to his face, "the God of your fathers spake unto me yesterday, saying: 'Take thou heed that thou speak not unto Jacob either good or bad.'"

Then fear fell from Jacob. That very night that he had driven sleep from his eyes and lain straining into the darkness, God had been across the valley, speaking to his old enemy, fast asleep in his tent, behind those same fires. Once again it crashed upon him: God had been in this place, and he had not known.

He stood up and told Laban the truth to his face.

"Because I was afraid: for I said, It may be thou wouldst take thy daughters from me. This twenty years have I been with thee; in the day the drought consumed me, and the frost by night; and my sleep departed from mine eyes. Thus have I been twenty years in thy house: I served thee fourteen years for thy two daughters, and six years for thy cattle; and thou hast changed my wages ten times. Except the God of my father, the God of Abraham, and the Fear of Isaac, had been with me, surely thou hadst sent me away now empty. God hath seen mine affliction, and the labour of my hands, and rebuked thee yesternight."

Even as he spoke, the dread came on Laban again, the dread that had come upon him in his tent last night. What was the use of armed men against a man who had the shadow of God's hand around him? What if Jacob, with that strange Power behind him, came against him in his anger?

"My son," said Laban, soothingly, "what should I do against my own flesh and blood? Are not thy wives my daughters, and thy sons my grandsons? Come now, let us make a covenant, I and thou."

Then Jacob took a stone, with the memory upon him of that other stone in the hollow of the hills at Bethel, and set it upright; and he called to his brothers-in-law, and they came down and each lifted a great stone and set it in its place. And when they had reared a great pile of stones they stood, Jacob on one side, and Laban on the other, and swore a lasting peace. And Laban said: "This heap is a witness between me and thee this day. The Lord watch between me and thee, when we are absent one from another. This heap be witness, and this pillar be witness, that I will not pass over this heap to thee, and that thou shalt not pass over this heap to me, for harm. The God of Abraham judge betwixt us." And Jacob swore by the Fear of his father Isaac.

Then Jacob offered a sacrifice, and he and his kinsmen ate together beside the memorial stone. They called it Mizpah, the Watch Tower. And early the next morning Laban rose up and kissed his daughters and his grandsons and blessed them, and struck his tents. Jacob stood on the ridge watching the troop file down the mountain pass with their faces to the east, and a great peace was in his heart. Then he turned and looked down the other side of the great ridge, to the Jordan and the hills beyond. Somewhere in the south the mountains of Edom rose red and green in the early sun. It was the country of Esau, his brother. And as he looked, he was afraid.

THEY came down the mountain passes of Gilead, riding in the shining weather. Gilead was the great spice garden of Palestine, and the sweetness of his own country clung about Jacob's heart. But there was fear in it too. Every step brought him nearer Esau, and the vengeance that had been brewing for twenty years. Up till now Jacob had been too busy with the fear of the danger behind him to think of the danger before: now he knew that this that was coming upon him was a worse thing. For Laban would have done no harm to Rachel and Leah and the children; they were of his own blood: but what mercy would Esau show to the wives of the man who had tricked him of the headship of the clan?

He sent messengers before him to find his brother in the red hills of Edom; for Esau had gone out into the mountains, and had won his own inheritance with his sword. They were to tell him how he had been with Laban, and had done well there; and now had sent "to tell my lord, that I may find grace in thy sight." In a few days the messengers came back. "My lord Esau said neither good nor bad; and behold, he cometh to meet thee, and four hundred men with him."

It was worse than he had feared: Esau alone was terrible enough; and what were the four hundred of his following but so many desert wolves? A fight did not bear thinking of: their only chance was in escape. Miserably he divided his huge defenceless caravan into two companies, thinking forlornly "While they are falling upon me, the other may get free." And then he bethought himself to pray. It was a desperate prayer; for the first time in his life Jacob realised that he had nothing to say for himself. "O God," he said, "I am not worthy of the least of all the mercies and of all the truth which Thou hast shewed unto Thy servant; for with my staff I passed over this Jordan, and now I am become two bands. Deliver me, I pray Thee, from the hand of my brother, from the hand of Esau; for I fear him, lest he will come and smite me, and the mother with the children."

So he ceased from praying: but there came no sign. There was no difference; no vision: around him the noises of the camp, and overhead the cheerful sun blazing in the blue emptiness of the sky. Jacob's swift brain fell to planning new ways. He went down among the herds, choosing out the best and likeliest of them, cattle and sheep and goats and camels and bulls and asses and foals, and divided them into droves, and started them off one behind the other. And to the drivers he said, "When Esau meets you, and asks, 'Whose are these, and where are they going?' say, 'These are thy servant Jacob's; it is a present sent unto my lord Esau; and behold, he is behind us.'" Surely, he said to himself, when he meets these time after time it will appease him, and afterward I shall see his face.

It was now near sunset. They were at the fords of Jabbok, a little river in a steep valley of oak and pine. It is not an easy ford, for the water is swift and deep, and Jacob busied himself sending Rachel and Leah and the children across, and the rest of the caravan, to encamp for the night on the farther side. The last of the droves had gone their way; the ford was left quiet and dark; and Jacob was there alone.

He was craving for it after the bustling, feverish day. He was worn out with planning and contriving and telling men what to say: the fever was in his brain. All that he had done and suffered and gained in twenty years was swinging on a knife-edge. He was face to face with it at last, the thing that he had run away from twenty years ago: it had waited for him. He had done all that a man could do, and he was helpless still. And then there came One out of the dark, and wrestled with him till the breaking of the day.

He did not know who it was; he could not see: he could only feel the strong grappling of the hands. All night he struggled with Him, and the Stranger had not prevailed. But even as the feeling of the dawn was in the air, and the hope grew in his heart that he might yet win through, the Stranger stretched out his hand and touched him on the thigh. It was only a touch, but Jacob lurched sideways, the strength gone from him. Who was This who had let a man wrestle with Him the night through, and could lame him with a touch of His finger when He pleased?

The Stranger had won, but He did not go. Jacob still clutched Him, but that could not hold Him, unless He chose to be held. At last He spoke, the first time that Jacob had heard His voice all night. "Let me go," He said, "for the day breaketh." Whether Jacob knew the voice or not, he could hardly tell; he was in a strange place, past all memory, and nothing of account but this Man whom he still firmly held. "I will not let Thee go," he said, "except Thou bless me."

"What is thy name?" said the Stranger. And Jacob answered Him with the meanness and the failure of his whole life on his lips: "The Supplanter."

"Thy name shall no more be called The Supplanter," came the answer, "but Israel, a prince of God: for as a prince hast thou power with God and with men, and hast prevailed." The words went through Jacob with the burning and the splendour of fire. From the shame and the meanness and the sin, "from the contagion of the world's slow stain," he was set free. It was Deliverance—from himself. And desire came on him to know for a surety his Deliverer. "Tell me, I pray Thee, Thy name," he asked Him. "Wherefore," questioned the voice, "dost thou ask after My name?" For a moment He lingered to bless him, and was gone.

And Jacob rose up, lame with the touch of that Hand upon him. And Jacob called the name of the place Peniel: "for I have seen God face to face, and my soul is restored." And as he passed over Peniel the sun rose upon him, and he halted upon his thigh.

TWELVE

THE air was clear, for it was early. One could see a great way off. Jacob, walking solitary by his slow-moving caravan, lifted up his eyes and saw a band of horsemen coming across the plain. They rode like men of the desert, and at the head of them he saw a single horseman, and he knew it for Esau his brother. The reckoning had come at last: and at last Jacob went to meet it face to face. Only for a moment he stopped, to alter a little the line of the caravan, and to see that Rachel was safe in the rear; and then he went on alone.

What was in Esau's mind as he rode at the head of his four hundred spears, whether it was vengeance for himself and spoil for his men that he saw in the great unwieldy caravan, no man knows. But as he watched, a solitary figure moved out from it, and came to meet him. It came slowly; and with a great rush of pity, Esau saw that his brother was lame. He got down from his horse and ran to him; Jacob could not run, but he limped on as quickly as he could, for he saw the look on Esau's face. The next moment Esau's great arms were about him, and the two clung together and cried.

And so there was kindness and forgiveness between them, and the long bitterness was healed. And for the second time Jacob found that in his weakness he had power with God and with men. Esau's face as he bent over him had something of the look that he had seen on that other face last night. "I have seen thy face," he said to Esau, "as though I had seen the face of God, and thou wast pleased with me." And they parted in peace.

This is not the end of the story of Jacob; but it is the end of the story of Jacob the Supplanter. The rest is a long story: how he went to Bethel and built a great altar in the hollow among the hills; how Rachel died, and he buried her, and wept for her; how his sons grew up wild and vexed his heart; how they sold Joseph for a slave, and for twenty years he mourned him as killed by the wild beasts, and how he found him a prince of Egypt; how Joseph sent for him, and he took his last journey there, and was brought into the presence of Pharaoh, and blessed him; and how he lived to see Joseph's sons before he died, and to lay his hands on their heads; but he summed it in that last blessing, "God, before whom my fathers Abraham and Isaac did walk, the God which fed me all my life long unto this day, the Angel which redeemed me from all evil, bless the lads."

He died in Egypt, and they brought him back and buried him in Abraham's cave at Hebron; and all he had in the land that God had promised him was a grave. Yet he died content; for he had seen a vision, and dreamed a dream.

The Story of

Saul the King

ONE

I WANT you to get a map of Palestine, not Palestine as it is now, but as it was in the old, old days before there were kings in Israel. And I want you to find a range of hills running south, through Mount Ephraim and Judah. Bethel is among those hills, where Jacob saw the vision of God, and so is Jerusalem: one of them is the Mount of Olives. All the story that I am going to tell you was lived amidst that range of hills, until it ended on the mountains of Gilboa in the north, and on the walls of the city of Bethshan.

There was no royal city then. Jerusalem was in the hands of the heathen; David was the first to take it, and David was not yet born. All down the sea coast was the country of the Philistines; every now and then they made raids into Palestine, and they had garrisons among the hills, in the very heart of the land. The only great man among the Hebrews was Samuel the Judge, and he was old. He lived in Ramah, on the slopes of these same hills, but every year he went on circuit. And the people said, "You are old, and we have no man to lead us. Give us a King."

"God is your King," said Samuel, and he was angry. But the people said, "We want a man. Give us a King to reign over us, like the Kings of the Philistines." Then Samuel went and prayed, for his heart was sore. And God said to him, "They are not tired of you; they are tired of Me. None the less, they shall have their way. Go home to Ramah, and one day I shall send you the man born to be King." So Samuel went home to Ramah, and waited for the coming of the King.

Now on the hills going south from Ramah there was a little country town; it was called Gibeah; afterwards, when it was famous, Gibeah of Saul. Two men lived there, brothers, and strong men of their hands; and one of them had a son. He stood head and shoulders above any man in all the countryside; and he was splendid in his going. They called him Saul; which means in Hebrew, The Desired.

But just now Saul was not in Gibeah. Two days ago he had set out with one of his father's servants to look for the asses. They had strayed, and strayed far. Saul struck out past Bethel into the hill country of Ephraim, but he did not find them. Two days he went among the hills, asking at all the hill farms, but heard no word of them. And on the morning of the third day Saul said, "Let us go back, for my father will not be worrying any more about the asses, but about us." And this was true, for there was a stronghold of the Philistines among the hills.

They had halted at the side of the road to eat their breakfast; it was the remains of the loaves in their wallets, and water from the well. The serving man was looking at the hill road, climbing up to a little white-walled town. "By the look of it," he said, "that should be Ramah. There is a great seer lives in Ramah. Let us go and ask him. It may be he will tell us where the asses are." Saul turned his wallet upside down. "And what will we give him for his trouble?" he said. "For we have eaten all the bread, and we cannot go without something in our hands." "I have the fourth part of a shekel of silver," said the serving man. "We will give him that." And so they went up the hill.

It was still early. As they climbed they met young girls coming down to the well, with water-pots on their heads. "Is the Seer here?" Saul asked them, and the girls said, wondering who the stately stranger might be, "He is. But make haste, for there is a sacrifice in the high place, and he goes to bless the feast; the people will not eat until he comes. Find him before he goes." So they went on, and reached the gate; and even as they went in, Samuel came through it alone.

They stopped and looked at each other. And in that moment it was shown to Samuel that this was the man born to be King.

They stood together, the last Judge and the first King of Israel, but Saul saw only a venerable old man. "Sir," he said, "tell me, I pray you, which is the Seer's house?"

"I am the Seer," said Samuel. "And now, go up before me into the high place, for you shall eat with me this day. And in the morning I will let thee go, and tell thee all that is in thine heart. The asses? Set not thy mind on them; for they are found." Saul stood bewildered. "And on whom," said Samuel gravely, "is the desire of Israel? Is it not on thee, and on thy father's house?"

"Sir," said Saul, "I am of the least of the tribes of Israel, and my father's house is the least of the tribe. Wherefore do you say these things to me?" Samuel made no answer, but when they came to the feast he set Saul in the place of the chief guest, and had him served with honour. All day the feast lasted. Saul sat among the elders of the city, very silent, but the stateliest there. And all day Samuel watched him, pondering in his heart.

At last, the feast was over, and Samuel brought Saul back to his own house: they went up to the housetop in the cool of the evening, and sat there, the old man and the young. It seemed to Saul that his heart lay before the eyes of this man as before the eyes of God; and he told him all the thoughts of his youth; of war with the Philistines and of winning a great name; and Samuel listened, and bade him sleep. So Saul lay down on the housetop, and slept under the stars.

About the spring of the day he heard the old man calling him. "Up," said Samuel, "for I will send thee away." They went out together through the sleeping streets, and through the gate into the freshness of the dawn. Then Samuel spoke. "Send thy servant on before us," he said, and waited till the sound of his footsteps was faint on the road. "And now," he said, "stand still, that I may shew thee the Word of God." Saul stood still. The old Judge raised his arm holding a horn of oil and poured it upon his head, as though he were anointing a priest to the service of the altar.

Then he kissed him in the homage of the East, as a man kisses the hand of the King.

"Is it not," he said, "that the Lord hath appointed thee to be prince over His people? And as thou goest from me, thou shalt be turned into another man. Behold, thou goest with God." He stood, watching Saul go downhill in the sunrise: and even as Saul turned his back to go from Samuel, God gave him another heart.

He came to roads that were strange no longer, but they were strange roads to him. They passed through the little country town of Gibeah, that was to be Gibeah of Saul, but he went in a dream. Suddenly a voice hailed him, and he woke with a start. His uncle, ploughing in the fields, left his yoke of oxen standing, and came down to the foot of the furrow. "Where were you this long time?" he asked. "I didn't see you."

"We went," said Saul slowly, "to look for my father's asses, and when we could not find them, we came to Samuel." There he stopped. His uncle eyed him curiously.

"And what might Samuel have to say to you?" he asked.

"He told us plainly," said Saul, "that the asses were found." His uncle grunted, and Saul went his way. He had spoken the truth about the asses, but of the finding of the kingdom he did not speak. It was too great.

T W O

IT WAS the spring of the year, and they were busy with the ploughing. Morning after morning Saul yoked his oxen, and followed them down the long furrows, and no one knew that the man behind the plough was the anointed King. But the thought of it kept with Saul; the grey dawn at the gate of Ramah, and they two standing in that lonely place; the strange kiss of homage from the man most feared in Israel, and that stranger moment thereafter when for the first time in his life he had felt the nearness of God.

The days went by, and Samuel made no sign. Then one night Saul came home, and found the place astir. There was a strange man by the fire, with the dust of long roads on him. Saul's father and his uncle were asking him questions.

"Mizpah is the place," said the man. "You mind where the big fight was? It is there the meeting is to be, and the word is for every tribe in Israel."

"What meeting?" said Saul.

The man looked up. "It is Samuel's word," he said, "and he has a 'Thus saith the Lord' behind it. It is a King he will be choosing, maybe, or else it is for arming the people against the trouble there is to be. For they do be saying that the men of Ammon are gathering up in the mountains, and it is on Gilead they will come first, and after that they will be over the river to us."

Saul looked at the ox-goad in his hands. "And this is what we will be fighting with," he said bitterly, "for the Philistines have left hardly a sword in the land."

Saul's uncle was watching him. "Had Samuel any word of the meeting when you were with him?" he asked.

"He had not," said Saul, and went out of the house. It was coming very near.

They gathered together to Mizpah, the "Watch Tower" of Benjamin, almost three thousand feet above the sea. There were men from every tribe, and some had come from far, and the baggage was piled in heaps round the place of meeting. Saul was with his father and his uncle, and the sound of the voices round him, laughing and arguing and shouting greetings, was a sound like the buzzing of flies high overhead in summer trees. There came a stirring in the crowd, and then a hush. Saul looked up. Samuel had come.

He stood for a while on the height beside the altar, looking down at the mass below. Then he began to speak. "Thus saith the Lord God," he said, and the words came like hammer strokes, "I brought you up from Egypt, and I Myself was your King. I was with you in battle, to deliver you from the hand of all kingdoms. But ye have this day rejected your God: ye have said, 'Give us a man to be our King.' You, then, come before the Lord, thousand by thousand, tribe by tribe."

The chiefs of the twelve tribes came near, and Samuel made ready to cast the lot. "It will be Judah," said Saul's father. "Do you remember what our father Jacob said when he was dying— 'The sceptre shall not depart from Judah'?"

"Maybe so," said Abner. But he was watching the face of Saul.

Again Samuel's voice struck the silence.

"It is the tribe of Benjamin," he said. "Let the tribe of Benjamin in its clans come near."

There was a stirring among the people, as the smallest tribe in Israel shouldered itself through the crowds. In the commotion Abner lost sight of Saul: when he looked for him again he was gone.

The lot was long in casting, but the silence was tense.

"It is the clan Matri," said Samuel. "Let the clan Matri come near."

There were not many, but they were men of their hands and good fighters.

"Are ye all here?" said Samuel, as he took note of them.

"There is the young man, Saul," said Abner. "He was here but now."

The silence fell again. Saul, hidden among the baggage, stood gripping a pack saddle with both hands. He had hidden, for he could not face it. What was he, to be King over all this host?

Again Samuel spoke. Saul's name came to him from a great way off. The blood was hammering in his ears, making him blind and deaf. There was a murmur of many voices talking at once, some angry, most of them simply curious. Saul leant forward, his head between his arms. What would he not give to be behind his oxen in this open weather, making slow furrows in the quiet ground? If he were a man, he told himself, he would go out and face them. But he was only a frightened child—a child playing hide-and-seek from a kingdom.

The minutes passed. A wild hope came on Saul. Perhaps they would not find him. They would tire of looking, and cast another lot. And in the twilight he would slip away home.

Then Samuel's voice came again. "Behold," he said, "he has hidden himself among the baggage."

In another moment he was taken. A great rush of men swept him through the crowd to the altar where Samuel stood, surging and ebbing round him. With a swing of his great shoulders Saul turned and faced them, head and shoulders above all the people. Samuel on the height looked down upon him standing there, with his look of the captured lion, and his heart yearned on him. So diffident and so mighty; what might his end be?

He turned to the people. "See ye him whom the Lord hath chosen, that there is none like him among all the people!"

For a moment there was silence, while they stood face to face, the people and the King. They gazed at the man, solitary before them, and conviction came upon them. It was true what

Samuel had said; among all the thousands of Israel, there was none like him. "By the splendour of God," they said in their hearts, "it is a *man!*"

Then suddenly, the cheering broke. "God save the King!" they shouted, the first time ever the cry was raised in Israel. Wave upon wave of it crashed on the man standing there, the only silent man in all those thousands, standing in the most awful loneliness he had ever known. The madness of a crowd had come upon them; they were yelling in a passion of adoration, men who a moment before had never seen his face. The world to Saul had become a sea of sound that roared in his ears and sent flashes of darkness across his eyes. He stood magnificently; only Samuel guessed something of his agony.

At last the cheering died. Once again Samuel stood forward to send away the people with his word of peace. To Saul, waiting, came a few score men to bring him on his way. But as he left the field a mass of malcontents were already drifting together. "This the King!" they sneered, as Saul passed by. "How shall this man save us?" But Saul held his peace.

THREE

I WANT you to get the map, and look for Gilead, the pleasant-est land in all Palestine. First of all find Gibeah of Saul in the middle range of hills. Now think of a little stony road, white with dust, skirting the foot of the hills, and go along that road for miles and miles, with the mountains on one side and the river on the other, till you come to the fortress of Bethshan. It was, you know, a stronghold of the Philistines, and on a clear morning one looked from it across the Jordan to a fair green lap of land, with a mountain range beyond it, and on the nearest spur of those mountains a little white-walled town. That was Jabesh-Gilead, the chief city of the great spice-gar-den; and the valleys of Gilead were the loveliest of all the valleys of Israel.

Now so far the Philistines had never crossed the river; but on the other side beyond the mountains, there were worse than they. The Philistines stood over Israel like a lion with one great paw on Bethshan, but over the mountains the men of Ammon prowled like hungry wolves. For a long time they had lurked behind the mountains; now they were into the valley like a river that has broken its dam, swept it in one great, cruel wave, and sat down before the walls of Jabesh-Gilead for a siege.

Now, the men of Jabesh-Gilead were a peaceful folk, and they were few. If they fought, they knew they would be beaten; and the men of Ammon had no mercy. It was well for the man who died in battle; it was not good to fall into their hands alive. Besides, there were the women and children.

They held a sorrowful council; and then sent out the elders of the city to Nahash, the Ammonitish King. "Make a treaty with us," they said, "and we will be your servants." The King looked at the old countrymen trembling before him, and he mocked them. "I will, indeed, make a treaty with you," he said, "and these will be the terms. Come out to me, and we will thrust out the right eye of every man among you. It will be a lesson to Israel."

The old men looked at one another. Israel? There was no Israel now. Once they had gone into battle together, like one man, but now it was every man for himself. Then they remembered the strange new business of the King, and a faint hope stirred. "Give us seven days," they said to Nahash, "and we will send messengers through all the coasts of Israel, and if there is no man to save us, then we will come out to thee."

They turned, and the King watched them go, like a cat watching its mouse. He knew it would be of no use; and he liked to think of their terror and their struggle these seven days. There was wailing in the little town when they came back, but in an hour swift runners went out from the gate and through the enemy lines and across the ford. They were going by the little hill road to find Gibeah of Saul.

They came to Gibeah of Saul in the late afternoon, and told their tidings, and the people wailed in the streets. "Where is the man that was made King?" the messengers asked, and when they heard that he was in the far pasture with the ploughing they looked at one another. "A fine King this," they said, and they thought of Nahash among his warriors, clad in shining armour, with the circle of gold about his head. That was something like a King. They stood about the doorpost, footsore and heartsick, and told awful tales of what the Ammonites had done in the valley, and the women cried out, and the children hid for fear. The ill news went from house to house, till the whole town was mourning as if a city were dead. And even as they stood, Saul came slowly up the road behind his oxen, his goad in his hand, and his head sunk on his breast. He was thinking long thoughts these days, wondering why Samuel had

ever chosen him, to send him back to the plough; wondering
if that dawn at Ramah had not been all a dream.

Suddenly the sound of the keening struck on his ears. He lifted
his head. "What ails the people?" he asked, and the women
wailed still louder and stood back that he might see the
strangers. They came out to meet him, and told him the miserable story. "Seven days he has given us, and at the end of
seven days we go to him and he thrusts out the right eye of every
man among us, that he may tell it for a shame upon Israel."

Saul listened, and as he listened there came upon him a
passion of anger and pity that was like the passion of God. It
bore him up like a spring tide. He had forgotten the fear and
the waiting and the doubt. He had seen the will of God: for
this cause was he born. In a flash he knew what he must do.
Words were not enough to rouse this people; he looked round
at the disheartened crowd, wailing afresh every time the messengers paused: chicken-hearted. Then he stooped to the hatchet
that lay by the doorpost for the cutting of wood, and with one
swing of his great arms he had stunned the ox beside him.
They ceased their keening, and watched him open-mouthed.
Then the second ox went down, and he fell to hewing them in
pieces like a man possessed. Then he turned to the crowd, and
flung a bleeding quarter into their midst. "Take each man of
you the like of it," he shouted, "and be gone into all the coasts
of Israel, and to every man you meet say, 'Whosoever cometh not
forth after Saul and after Samuel, so shall it be done to his oxen!'"

For a moment they stood amazed; then with a yell they
surged round him for his orders. That night the news of it went
through Israel like the sending of the Fiery Cross. On the sixth
day Saul stood at Bezek, below the heights of Bethshan, and
numbered the men who had come to him: thirty thousand from
Judah, from Israel three hundred thousand. He turned from
them to the messengers: "Say ye to the men of Jabesh-Gilead.
'To-morrow, by the time the sun is hot, ye shall have help.'"

There was joy in Jabesh-Gilead when the messengers came back. Once again they sent their embassy to the King of Ammon. "Sir," they said, "to-morrow we will come out to you, and you shall do with us all that seemeth good to you." They came back humbly to the city, and the men of Ammon jeered as they went by and promised them what they would suffer on the morrow. That night the King sat late, carousing with his captains; the men-at-arms drank in their tents, boasting of the morrow, of the spoil of the rich little city. The watch-fires sank lower, and at last even the sentries slept.

Meantime through the darkness there came a great host. From under the walls of Bethshan to the fords of Jordan, and across the fords in the darkness to the city of Jabesh-Gilead, they marched, with their King at their head. Never in all Saul's life was he to know a night so splendid as this of his first command. Once again he was to come at dead of night from the walls of Bethshan to Jabesh-Gilead, but that night was hidden from his eyes. That was Saul's last march; this was his first.

The word was given at dawn. Waking in the ghastly blue light the men of Ammon heard the war-cry, "For Saul and Samuel," and rushed out, stumbling over their own men, to find the enemy in the very heart of the camp. From dawn to daylight, from daylight to the heat of noon the men of Israel slew, and by evening there were not two of the Ammonites left together. The people were mad with victory. When Saul came before them, they met him with a great shout, "Where are the men that said, 'Shall Saul reign over us?' Bring them out, and we will put them to death."

Saul lifted his hand. "There shall not a man be put to death this day," he said, "for to-day the Lord hath wrought salvation in Israel."

"Come," said Samuel, "let us go to Gilgal, and renew the kingdom there." And all the people went to Gilgal, and there they crowned Saul King before the Lord.

FOUR

IT WAS two years since Saul had stood beside Samuel on the height at Gilgal, and heard Samuel's great charge to the people and their King; for two years he had been King of Israel. He had grown used to it. The glory and the terror had gone from it. When the people shouted "God save the King!" it did not waken any more the old wild craving for God's hand to be indeed upon him. He was not helpless any more; he did not wonder any more that God had chosen him. He had found himself; he knew that he was a King after the people's heart. Sometimes he remembered even yet the terror of the moment when the thunder crashed overhead in a smiling sky, the day of his crowning, and the people shuddered and prayed; or the stranger shadow that fell on him when Samuel ended his charge —"The Lord will not forsake His People, for His great name's sake; because it hath pleased Him to make you His people . . . only fear the Lord and serve Him with all your heart. . . . But if ye shall still do wickedly, ye shall be consumed, both ye and your King."

It was the time of the wheat harvest, yet even in the heat of noon, Saul had felt strangely chilled. Long since the fear had left him. He was sure of himself.

Then came the Philistine invasion. For a long time they had been content to stand sentinel over Israel like an armed guard. But Jonathan, Saul's son, was tired of that bondage; tired of seeing his people cowering like mice in their holes. He took the thousand men that his father the King had given him, and fell on one of the hill forts and took it by storm. The news rang through Israel and Philistia. Saul blew the trumpet for the gathering of the people, for he knew that the gauntlet was

flung. From all over Israel they crowded to him at Gilgal, praising Jonathan, but in their hearts was fear. For they said, "It is
ill work rousing a hornet's nest."

And the hornets were indeed aroused. "It is time," said the
lords of the Philistines, "that these Hebrews were taught a lesson."
They gathered themselves together, thirty thousand chariots of
war and six thousand cavalry, infantry like the sand of the sea,
and poured into Benjamin, taking their stand on the heights of
Michmash. As for the country folk, they scattered like rabbits
before them, hiding in caves and thickets and dens. Some fled
across the river to the pleasant green valleys of Gilead, and the
few hundreds of fighting men gathered trembling about Saul.

Now, at the first tidings, a message came to Saul. "Thou shalt
go down before me to Gilgal," said Samuel, "and I will come
after thee, to offer burnt-offerings. Seven days shalt thou tarry
till I come to thee, and shew thee what thou shalt do."

"Seven days," thought Saul to himself, "and every moment
precious." He was not any longer a child, to wait at every step
for Samuel to tell him the will of God. He was a man grown,
and a King. Day after day Saul waited, brooding. Every day
scared men came into the camp telling of the wonderful array
of the Philistines, of the cruel sharp blades on their chariot
wheels, of the havoc they were making of the countryside; and
every night deserters slipped away from the camp, some into
hiding on the hills of Ephraim, some even to the camp of the
Philistines. At first the army had numbered three thousand; at
roll call on the seventh day six hundred answered to their names.
Once, if Saul had remembered it, three hundred men under
Gideon had gone against the whole might of Midian, and
routed it; but Saul had forgotten. He stood looking up the
road to the hills with angry, desperate eyes. "Am I to wait here,"
he said to himself, "till the Philistines come down from Michmash and swamp us? The old man is right enough: we can't
go into battle without offering sacrifice. But what is the use of

waiting for him to shew me what is to be done? I see it well
enough myself." All day he waited, restless and chafing, watching the hill road. At sundown he turned to the priests: "Bring
the burnt-offerings to me," he said, and summoned the rem-
nants of his army. Glad, but ill at ease, the men crowded together; glad, that there was to be something doing at last; ill
at ease, because they had never yet gone into battle without a
"Thus saith the Lord" behind them. The King himself stood in
Samuel's place at the altar; the priests slew and offered the
sacrifice, and the smoke curled slowly up. Silence had fallen on
the men, when suddenly one from the look-out post came running.

"Is it the Philistines are upon us?" said Saul.

"Sire," said the man, "it is my lord Samuel."

"Stay here," said Saul to the troops. "Myself will go to meet
him."

Silently Saul went out along the darkening road. Behind him
the smoke of the altars hung in the quiet air. He went bravely,
but in his heart he was afraid. Samuel had halted when he
saw the stalwart figure coming through the dusk; his eyes had
gone beyond Saul, beyond even the smoke of the burnt-offerings. The words of greeting that Saul had been preparing died
on his lips. What was it that Samuel saw?

At last Samuel spoke. "What is this that you have done?" he
asked, and Saul's heart sank, for there was no anger in the voice,
but only a terrible regret.

"It was like this," began Saul desperately. "The men were
deserting, and the seven days were nigh over, and you had not
come. And there were the Philistines gathering at Michmash.
And I said to myself, the Philistines will come down upon me
and I have made no offerings. So I forced myself, and offered the
sacrifice myself."

Samuel stood listening, gazing with those steady eyes past
all the excuses into something that Saul could not see. "Thou
hast done foolishly," he said, and it seemed to Saul that the few

words stripped his soul bare. "Thou hast not done the will of God."

"For this cause was he born"—the memory of that great conviction came back to Saul, the day that he was empty of himself, and filled with the passion of God. For this cause was he King, that he might do the will of God. And he had not done it.

"It would have been," Samuel went on, with that same gentle sadness, "that you and your sons were Kings over Israel for ever; but now it will end with you. Already has God chosen Him a man after His own heart, to be captain over His people. Because you knew the will of God, and did it not."

Then Samuel turned and went his way to Gibeah, back to the hills of Benjamin. And Saul mustered his six hundred, and went after.

FIVE

SAUL was back among the mountains. There was a ridge of hills to the north, and a ridge of hills to the south, and a steep valley between. On one side the Philistines were encamped; on the other Saul, with his poor six hundred. Saul's tent was under a pomegranate tree, near where a landslip had been. Every day he saw the raiding parties go out from the Philistine camp, and every night he saw them come home down the valley below him, shouting and singing, and laden with their booty; and the fires of little ruined hill farms were red on the sky behind them. Saul's anger was black and bitter, but he dared not stir. He had lost his faith in himself, and he was in ill humour with God.

But Jonathan wearied of the long, dead days. He had climbed one morning to a sharp point of rock that was called "The Thorn" at the very end of the ridge, and he stood there looking across at the rock over the way; it was called "The Shining One" because of the glittering rock; it was the farthest outpost of the Philistines. He could see now and then a glint of armour. Suddenly he turned to his armour-bearer.

"Come," he said, "let us go over to these uncircumcised; it is nothing to God to save, by many or by few."

"I am with you," said his armour-bearer.

"See," said Jonathan, "I am going to show myself boldly, and challenge them. And if they say 'Wait till we come down to you,' we will not go. But if they say 'Come up,' we will go. It will be a sign that God has given them into our hands."

They scrambled down through the brushwood at the foot of the rock, and suddenly stood up clear, and shouted a challenge. Above on the narrow ledge they saw heads peering over, and jeering.

"Look!" said one to the other, "here be the Hebrews crawled out of their holes at last! Come up!" they shouted. "Come up, and we will show you something." Jonathan turned his head. "Come," he said softly, "it is the sign."

The rock was steep, and the two were hidden at the foot. Up the steepest face of it Jonathan went, climbing on his hands and knees, and his armour-bearer after him. The top of the rock was a narrow ledge, and there the Philistines hung about, chatting. "The mice have crept back to their holes again," they said, and laughed. And suddenly Jonathan was over the edge and upon them. Man after man they went down before that terrific onset, for there was no room to fight abreast; and whoever escaped Jonathan, the armour-bearer slew. Twenty men fell in a space like the furrow of a half-acre field, and the cry went through the camp that a great army of the Hebrews was upon them, and had taken them unawares. Panic came on the camp, a terror like the terror of God. They fell to hewing each other in their madness; and when Saul's sentries heard the outcry and looked they saw a great host streaming down the valley, men and horses, trampling each other in their fear.

"Who has gone from us?" said Saul. Hastily they called the roll, and Jonathan was not there, nor his armour-bearer. Then Saul blew the trumpet; down poured the six hundred from their stronghold, wild for battle; the sound of it rang through the valleys, and men in hiding burst from their dens and caves to follow after Saul. The Hebrew deserters in the Philistine camp rallied to the old standard, and turned against their flying masters. So the tide of battle rolled to Beth-Aven.

The battle-fury was on Saul again. It was good to be King, to be his own man again. "Hear me," he shouted to his men-at-arms, just as they surged to the attack, "the curse of God upon any one of you that stops to eat food until the evening. So shall I be avenged of my enemies!" It was a mad vow, and there was small thought of God in it. It was *his* enemies Saul was thinking of, and not God's. And God took him at his word.

All day the fight went on. At first the men went furiously with small thought of eating or drinking. But it was a long pursuit; morning wore to noon, and noon to the weary afternoon, and still they followed and slew. The first frenzy was gone; they felt sick and faint. Still they went stumbling on, through woods and stony watercourses, till the yellow afternoon sunlight grew dark before their eyes. Jonathan, among the foremost, was dizzy with the fight. He had not heard his father's vow, and he was sick with lack of food. They had passed into the shadow of a wood out of the glare of the sun, and as he went under a tree he saw where the wild bees had hived, and yellow honey trickling down the trunk. Without a thought he tasted it, and it brought back the light to his eyes. But a cry rose up behind him.

"Oh, my lord!" said one of his soldiers desperately, "thy father has put the curse on any who eats this day."

Jonathan set his mouth.

"Then," said he, "my father has done hurt to Israel. I did but taste the honey, and my sight is back to me. If the people had had leave to eat as they went, there would have been a slaying of Philistines this day." On he went, and the weary men behind him, faint but dogged. They had reached the valley of Aijalon; already it lay in shadow; but the sunset was red on the armour of the last of the Philistines vanishing over the ridge. Another moment and the sun had set.

With a great cry the starving men flung themselves on the spoil, killing and tearing and eating. Not one of them had a thought for the retreating enemy. Only Saul on the ridge above the valley gazed longingly after them, and cursed the men who could not fast for a day. He himself was drunk with victory. The stars were coming out one by one in the green-gold eastern sky; below him the camp fires twinkled out, and the smell of roasting flesh was in the air. Soon the moon would be up; if these below had but filled themselves the chase might go on all night, and not a Philistine be left to see the morning.

He shouted down to them, and they answered him with a cheer. "Sire," said the priest beside him. Saul turned half angrily.

"Were it not well," said the priest, "to ask counsel of God?" Saul checked himself.

"It is well minded," he said. "Ask of Him whether I shall go after the Philistines to-night; and if He will give them into our hands."

The priest vanished into the darkness. In a while he came back, with fear on his face.

"There is no answer," he said, trembling.

Saul stood, thinking swiftly. Someone had sinned that day, and God was angry. Who was it? He had it. Someone had broken his vow.

"Let the people come near," said Saul. They stood below him, a great dim mass in the twilight.

"There is sin among us," said Saul, "and whoever it be, though it be Jonathan my son, he shall surely die."

A shiver ran through the people, for they knew it was indeed Jonathan, but they said no word.

"I will cast lots," said Saul. "Stand you on that side, and Jonathan and I stand here."

"As you will," said the people, but it seemed a groan. For they loved Jonathan.

Saul stood with the lot in his hand. For a moment he looked up into the silent sky.

"Lord God of Israel," he said, "give a perfect lot." Then he threw it. It was for himself and Jonathan. Saul turned to the priest.

"Cast lots," he said harshly, "between me and Jonathan." The lot fell, and Jonathan was taken.

"Tell me what thou hast done, Jonathan," said Saul.

"I did but taste a little honey," said Jonathan. It was a young voice, and it broke a little. "And lo, I must die."

Saul listened stonily. So this was what his vow had come to. It was pride and not religion had made him make it. And God was punishing him. Very well, then. Saul hardened his heart.

"God do so, and more also," he said harshly, "for thou shalt surely die, Jonathan."

The silent mass below him in the dark broke into one shout of indignation.

"Shall Jonathan die, who hath wrought this great salvation in Israel? God forbid. As the Lord liveth, there shall not be a hair of his head fall to the ground; for he hath wrought with God this day."

Saul turned sullenly, and went to his tent. His secret heart was rejoicing over Jonathan, but there was a slow defiance in his heart. Someone had sinned that day, and God was angry. If it was not Jonathan—then who?

SIX

STILL Saul reigned King over Israel, and still he went out to battle, and won great glory. East and west and south he went, against Moab and Ammon and Edom and the Kings of Zobah and the Philistines. The land grew rich with spoil, and the old steading in Gibeah was become a King's household. God's hand was still upon him for good. He was still the man born to be King.

But to the south of Judah there lay a tribe, the cruellest of all. Hundreds of years before, when the Hebrews were escaping from Egypt, a great helpless caravan with women and little children, the men of Amalek came down from the mountains of Arabia and harried them in the desert. Ever since they had been the bitterest enemies of Israel, with a bitterness that never slept. And they were an evil people, and as cruel as they were evil. For a long time God had borne with them, but at last the cup of their iniquity was full, and He gave doom against them.

So there came a day that Samuel appeared again before Saul.

"Have you mind," he said, "of the day that the Lord God sent me to anoint you King over Israel?"

Saul inclined his head.

"Then hear," said Samuel, "for the Lord hath sent me yet again. Thus saith the Lord God, 'Go and smite Amalek, and utterly destroy all that they have. Everything that is in the land ye shall destroy, the men and the spoil together. Let no booty cleave to your hand, for ye are servants of the doom of God.'"

So Saul numbered the people, an exceeding great army, and marched to the south. But to the Kenites who lived among the men of Amalek he sent warning privately, that they might escape away, for they were kindly people. And when the Kenites had fled, Saul cried a Ban upon the men of Amalek, and swept through

the country with sword and fire. From Havilah in the east to
Shur in the west, in the way as you go down to Egypt, he rav-
aged, and when he ceased from slaughter, there was not a living
soul in all the land.

It was a wealthy tribe, wealthy in cattle and sheep. Saul
looked at the great droves, and grudged the thought of losing
them.

"It is surely enough," he argued with himself, "that we have
slain the people of the land. That is the Doom of God. But what
harm might there be in keeping a few of these? It would be a
poor thing to go back empty as when we came. The best of
them we will keep, and some of them we will sacrifice to the
Lord in Gilgal. He cannot be ill-pleased."

So he went out, and the people heard him joyfully, for they
coveted the booty. Slowly they came back to Gilgal, for they
must time their march to the slow-moving herds. Behind them
the land of Amalek lay black and smouldering under the eye of
the sun, and no living creature stirred in it. But the men who
had done judgment upon it came back, not like God's avengers,
but laden like common thieves. God had called a crusade; they
had turned it into a cattle-drive.

Meantime Samuel waited in Ramah. Day and night he prayed
for Saul, for the hope was in his heart that this time he would
obey, and God be very gracious to him. For Samuel loved him,
and for all his pride and his high hand he remembered the
young man Saul who had come seeking his father's asses, and had
talked with him all night long. But one night even as he prayed
there came the word of the Lord to Samuel, saying, "It repenteth
Me that I have set up Saul to be King, for he hath turned back
from following Me." Then Samuel cried to the Lord all night
for Saul, but there came no answer. Early in the morning he
rose and went to find him.

The people directed him upon the roads. Saul, they said, was
even now come to Gilgal. There went Samuel. The news was

brought to Saul, and he came out along the road to meet him. This time there was no shadow on his face. He had argued himself into thinking that he had done all that a wise man should, and he was confident with success.

"Blessed be thou of the Lord," he hailed him. "I have done what the Lord commanded me."

Samuel stood still. The camp was out of sight, but up from the plain below came the fitful bleating of sheep.

"Then," said Samuel, "what means this bleating of sheep in mine ears and the lowing of oxen which I hear?"

Saul stiffened himself. "They have brought them from the Amalekites," he said hardily. "The people spared the best of the sheep and the oxen to sacrifice to the Lord thy God. The rest we have utterly destroyed." He turned as if to bring Samuel on his way to the camp, but Samuel did not move.

"Stay," he said, "and I will tell thee what the Lord hath said to me this night."

"Say on," said Saul. They stood in the road together face to face, even as they had stood that other morning when Samuel anointed him in the dawn outside Ramah. The memory of it was with them both, and it was of it that Samuel spoke first.

"Saul," he said, "when you were little in your own sight, were you not made head of the tribes of Israel, and the Lord anointed you King over Israel? And the Lord sent you on a journey and said, 'Go and utterly destroy the sinners the Amalekites, and fight against them till they be consumed'? Why then did you not obey the voice of the Lord, but flew upon the spoil, and did evil in His sight?"

"I did obey the voice of the Lord," said Saul stubbornly, "I did go the way that He sent me. I did utterly destroy the Amalekites. But the people took the spoil, the best of the sheep and oxen, to sacrifice them to the Lord in Gilgal."

"Does God care for meat offerings or for obeying Him?" asked Samuel. "To obey is better than sacrifice, and to listen to Him better than the fat of rams. For rebellion is as the sin of witchcraft, and stubbornness is as idolatry. Because thou hast rejected the word of the Lord, He hath also rejected thee from being King."

Saul's defence broke.

"I have sinned," he said. "I have disobeyed the command of the Lord and the words you said. It was because I feared the people. So now, I pray you, pardon my sin, and turn again with me, that I may worship the Lord."

The hope left Samuel's heart as he listened. This Saul was gone very far from the Saul he knew. Did he think one could juggle with the will of God?

"I will not return with thee," he said, more hardly than he had ever spoken. "Thou hast rejected the word of the Lord, and the Lord hath rejected thee from being King over Israel." And he turned to go.

Saul, desperate, sprang to stay him, and caught the old man's cloak. So fiercely he clutched it that it rent, and he stood with the fragment in his hand.

"Even so," said Samuel, "hath the Lord rent the kingdom from thee, and given it to a neighbour of thine that is better than thou. And the Strength of Israel will not lie or repent."

Saul's short frenzy was spent. He stood gazing at Samuel.

"I have sinned," he pleaded. "Yet I pray you turn with me. Honour me before the people. Turn with me that I may worship God."

So Samuel turned with Saul. Together they stood before the altar at Gilgal, as on the day of his crowning. And only they two knew that the crown was taken from him, and that Saul was no longer Saul the King. Then Samuel went to Ramah, and Saul to his own stead that was already called Gibeah of Saul. And Samuel came no more to see Saul until the day of his death. None the less he mourned for him, and his mourning came before God.

SEVEN

IT WAS not until Samuel had gone from him that the blackness came upon Saul. There had been the stir of the sacrifice, and he and the chiefs had brought Samuel on his way with leave takings. Samuel had kept his word: there was no sign from him that Saul was no more King. For Saul himself, he dared not think on it. For the last time Samuel and he went down the road together, and then took leave. Saul stood to watch the old Judge going away from him into the twilight. It seemed to him that half his life went with him. It was Samuel who had brought him to a high place where the glory of God shone upon his head, and the praise of men swept him like a warm wind; and now Samuel had gone and left him alone, and in a dark place. For a long time there had been a cloud between him and the glory overhead, but to-night there was a blackness.

It came nearer and nearer in his tent. Over and over again the words of Samuel droned in his ear. "Because thou hast rejected the word of the Lord, He also hath rejected thee from being King." Other words there were, about the kingdom being given to a man better than he, "a neighbour of thine that is better than thou . . . a neighbour of thine that is better than thou." Once it had been, "See ye him whom the Lord hath chosen, that there is none like him among all the people?" but now there was someone better than he. So high a thing it was, this matter of the kingdom; and he had failed it. It was like a full cup put into his hand, and he had carried it with his head high, proud of the splendour and the shining of it. But the water that was in the cup was the will of God; and that water he had spilled on the ground. "Because thou hast rejected the word of the Lord, He also hath rejected thee. . . . He also hath rejected thee."

It did not end so. God's judgment was on Saul the King; His mercy waited for Saul the man. But to Saul in his dumb anguish it was all one. It was his pride that was wounded, wounded to death. To have lost the kingdom was as though he had lost his soul.

Dawn came, and the waking of the camp, and he roused himself and gave orders for the march home to Gibeah, Gibeah of Saul. There the slow days went by, and no word came from Samuel in Ramah. The cloud lifted a little; there were days when Saul held his court and took counsel with Abner and his captains, not unlike the Saul of old. But there were other days when the blackness fell, and it could no longer be hid. On those days no man saw the King, and his great spear thrust at the door of his tent was a barrier that none dared to pass. Only the captains spoke together and said, "It is an evil spirit from God."

Once, when the blackness for a moment lifted, they spoke to him, greatly daring.

"Sire," they said, "it is an evil spirit from God that troubleth thee. Now if it please thee, let us look for a man that can play the harp; for the sound of the harp shall charm the spirit from thee, and thou shalt be well."

Saul looked up with a gleam of hope, for he feared the coming of the blackness as he feared nothing in the world.

"Know you of any?"

"Sire," said one of the young men, "there is a lad in my own country, a herd of the sheep, David, the son of Jesse."

"Let you bring him," said the King, and sent his messengers. But long before they reached the hill farm above Bethlehem the darkness had fallen again.

All day Abner stood at the door of the King's tent to keep guard. The sun blazed overhead, but there was no sound in the camp. It was as though a great evil bird had come, and hung brooding over it. The day wore to noon, and noon to afternoon, and still Abner watched. Then a great way off came one riding, and another on foot beside him, the sun glinting ruddy on his head. They came nearer. Young and fair faced he was; there was a harp slung on his shoulder, and he had twisted blue lilies round it, lest the strings should snap in the heat. To Abner's sun-dazed eyes the dew lay on him and on them.

"God be with you, my son," he said. "Go in to him yonder." He pulled up the huge spear that guarded the entrance, and David passed in. The folds of the tent dropped behind him, and darkness fell with it.

It was a long time before David saw the King. He stood by the middle of the tent, his great arms hanging on the cross beams, gazing straight into blackness. David knelt, but there was no sight in those eyes.

For a long while David knelt, afraid to stir. Then a strong pity for the King so great and so desolate came on him, and he thought on what he might play to bring him back from that dark place where his soul wandered. He untwined the blue lilies, and laid them on the withered grass at his feet, and then began to play. Slow, soft airs at first, airs that he played at the folding of the sheep, when one by one they came from the dewy pastures, and the stars came out in the sky; then the tune that brought the quails flying low about his feet, calling softly to their mates in the long grass; the song that the reapers sing, when the poppies are red in the corn; songs of the grape-gatherers, and songs of the marriage feast; the song of marching men on the roads. Last he played the great chant of the priests when the censers swing before the altar, but at that Saul stirred and moaned.

Then David left playing the songs that he knew of the people, and played his own thoughts, striving to make Saul see the things that he saw, beyond the stifling darkness of the tent. And while he played he sang: of the freshness of woods and of running water, and the burning of the sun on desert sand, and of swift flight of eagles in the air; of the goodness of living and the glory of it, of the feeling of water and sunlight and wind; of the crash and the splinter of spears, and the voices of men, shouting for Saul the King. Then he ceased, for a great shudder went through the tent, and Saul groaned, like a man who has wakened to torment.

For a while David sat perplexed, the harp silent under his hand. Then very slowly he began to play. It was a song that had come to him one morning as he went before his sheep to the pasture, and the thought of God came up about his heart. Twice he played the air before he sang the words, and the very music of it availed with Saul. The strain of his shoulders relaxed, and he stood leaning like a man sorely tired.

"The Lord is my Shepherd," David sang, but in the Hebrew it is more gracious.

> "The Lord is my Shepherd:
> I shall not want,
> He maketh me to lie down in green pastures;
> He leadeth me beside the still waters:
> He restoreth my soul."

Slowly peace came upon Saul. The weariness and fever and fret faded from him. For a moment he saw the great blue mountains that lie about every man's road, the mountains that are the thoughts of God concerning him. Very dim and very far it was, but he saw it—that to restore a man's soul is to restore him all things.

"God be with you, my son," he said, and went out like one set free.

EIGHT

THERE is a valley in Judah to the south of Bethlehem: a wide valley, with the stony bed of a brook in the middle of it, that was a river in the time of the rains. Here the Philistines had come, and pitched their camp along the southern ridge; Saul and his men stood to the defence on the northern ridge, and the valley was between. Once Saul would have stormed across the valley and up the slope, but that day was past. Day after day they lay there, and no one stirred. For this was a fight like no other fight. The Philistines had sent a challenge, and no man in Israel dared take it up. It was to be a fight between champions, and Israel had none.

He came every morning down the valley, Goliath of Gath; nine feet nine inches in height, with helmet and coat of mail, and a spear like a weaver's beam. He stood in face of the army and shook his spear and shouted, "Give me a man that we may fight together. I defy the armies of Israel this day." There came no answer from the ranks before him. Once he charged up the slope, and the men broke rank and ran like sheep. Saul knew it, and sickened with shame.

Then one day there came a shepherd boy over the hills from Bethlehem. He passed the sentries and came through the camp, asking for his brothers. He had creels on his back, and the men sniffed the warm smell of new-baked bread, and teased him for a loaf, and sent him on to the front line. Abner, the captain of the host, met him, and nodded very kindly, for Abner had a very soft heart for the boy who had cured the King.

"That is a great load you have," he said. "It is your brothers will be glad to see you. Are you come for good?"

"It is not that," said David. "My father is needing me for the sheep. But he was wearying to hear of them, so he sent me with the new-baked bread and a cheese for the captain of the company."

"And yourself was not sorry for the chance?" said Abner.

"I was not," said David; "I wanted to see the fight."

"I wish there was more to see," said the old general sourly, and left him.

There was a great shout in the front line when young David appeared. His three big brothers kept him down at home, but they were hungry for his news and his loaves, and while they ate and shared with the rest, David wandered round talking to everybody, for he was as friendly as a young dog. Suddenly there came a shout from the valley. Silence fell on the camp, a stillness and a fear. David turned and looked, listening till the great bull-voice roaring in the valley had ceased. But when he turned again, there was no fear on his face, but a great light of anger. "It is a shame upon us," he cried. "Who is that Philistine that he should defy the armies of God?"

Eliab, his eldest brother, scowled on him. "Is it for you to be talking?" he said. "Away home to your handful of sheep in the wilderness. It was the pride of your heart brought you here to see the fight."

"What have I done?" asked David, puzzled. Eliab turned away, black at heart that it was David and not he who had shown no fear.

David's voice had carried far. All over the camp men spoke to each other, chuckling over the courage of the youngster who had seen Goliath, and was not afraid. Abner heard it, and came with the story to Saul where he sat gloomy in his tent.

The King looked up. "Bring him to me," he said. "I would like well to see him again."

They brought David in. The King and he had become great friends before the war broke out, and David's father had sent for him to come home and mind the sheep, now that his brothers had to go.

"What is this you are saying about the man who has them all in fear?" asked Saul, very indulgently. But David was in deadly earnest.

"Sir," he pleaded, "let me go and fight him, and they need not be in fear any more."

Saul looked down at him from his great height.

"Child," he said, "what are you but a boy? What would you do against the Philistine that has been a man of war from his youth?"

"Sir," said David, "I used to be in the fields keeping my father's sheep; and there came a lion once, and stole a lamb and went off with it in his mouth: and I went after him and hit him, and he dropped the lamb and reared himself up against me, and I caught him by the beard and hit him again, and killed him. And I killed a bear. And this Philistine is no better than they, for he has defied the armies of God."

There was silence in the tent. Saul had forgotten how weak a man must be who fought against God. It was this boy who reminded him.

"Sir," went on David, and the pride had gone out of his voice, "the Lord that delivered me out of the paw of the lion and out of the paw of the bear, He will deliver me out of the hand of this Philistine."

Saul raised his hand. "Go," he said solemnly, "and the Lord go with thee."

David turned to the door of the tent. "Wait," said Saul. And while David stood amazed, the King stripped off his coat of mail, and put it on David with his own hands. The King's own helmet was set upon his head; the King's own sword was slung at his side. "Now," said Saul, and David swung forward. But the massive armour clanked about him, and hampered him.

"I cannot go in these," he said simply. "I have not proved

them." He laid them down, and passed out in his shepherd's tunic, with the wallet on his back, and his sling coiled up in his hand. Down the stony slope he went, while the whole army held its breath. He stooped for a moment at the brook; they saw him choosing five smooth stones as unconcernedly as if it were for a day's hunting; then he straightened himself, and crossed to the farther side.

The Philistine came pacing down the slope. David went steadily on. The Philistine halted and stared at him. Who was this child they had sent to fight him, with a stick in his hand, and a face as smooth as a girl's? For a full minute he gaped: then he found his voice, and cursed David for his impudence by all his gods. Still David came on.

"Come along," shouted the Philistine. "There will be good picking for the ravens off thy bones this night."

David halted.

"Thou comest to me with a sword, and with a spear, and with a shield," he said, "but I come to thee in the name of the Lord of hosts, the God of the armies of Israel, whom thou hast defied. This day will the Lord deliver thee into my hand."

With a roar the Philistine put down his head and charged. David came running lightly, slipping the stone into the sling. Still he ran: suddenly the sling whirled round his head, and the stone flashed through the air. Fair in the middle of the giant's forehead it sank; and he crashed to the ground like the falling of a tree.

Still David ran, till he stood beside him. He had no sword, but with both hands he tugged at the great hilt in the Philistine's scabbard. With Goliath's own sword he hewed off the mighty head, and holding it, turned to face his people.

The silence snapped in a tempest of cheering. Down they came like a river in spate, yelling destruction to the Philistines. The enemy ranks broke and fled, leaving tents and spoil, and neither side stopped nor stayed till they crossed the border. Great was the slaughter and the booty. For David, he came before Saul, with the great head still in his hand. Jonathan stood behind his father's chair.

"My son," said Saul, "thou shalt no more go home to thy father's house. Stay with us."

David stood still in his shabby tunic, and gazed at them both. Jonathan stepped down.

"It is my brother you will be," he said, and he flung round David's shoulders the cloak of the King's son. And the soul of Jonathan was knit with the soul of David, and Jonathan loved him as his own soul.

NINE

THE great campaign was over, and the army came home. Saul went with David beside him, for there was no jealousy in him; he loved him as one good soldier loves another. They had left the enemy's country, and were on their own familiar roads; the women in the little country towns came out to meet them at the word of their coming, with songs and dances; and the men straightened themselves and marched more proudly. Saul looked down at David, keeping step beside him. "It will be new to you, David," he said smiling. "It is an old story to me; listen!"

"Saul hath slain his thousands!" the women cried, and clashed their cymbals. Saul smiled upon them as he passed, for though it was an old story a man does not soon tire of it.

"Saul hath slain his thousands!" they sang again, and then their eyes caught the young champion who walked beside the King, the slayer of Goliath of Gath.

"Saul hath slain his thousands!" the first chorus chanted. "And David his ten thousands!" answered the second, and again the cymbals clashed. They did not mean disloyalty. It is the Eastern trick of the crescendo. But a sleeping evil thing, coiled in the King's brain, roused itself and struck at his heart.

"What is it, Sire?" asked David.

"Nothing," said the King; but he spoke no more that day. "They have given me but thousands," he said to himself, "and to him they have given tens of thousands: what can he have more but the kingdom?" Back it came, the weary refrain that always brought madness with it—"A neighbour of thine that is better than thou, a neighbour of thine that is better than thou."

The next morning they came for David in haste. "The King's malady is again upon him," they said, "but not as it was. Now he raves in the midst of the house." David, fearless, went to the presence, and found the King insane. Once again he began to play, and for a time the King was quiet, listening, his javelin in his hand. Slowly Saul's reason came back again; but with his waking came the knowledge that this, the only man he had to stand between him and the horror of darkness, was the man who was to take the kingdom from him. With a great and bitter cry he flung the spear. David swerved and fled from his face.

When Saul came to himself, it was to shame. He could not bear to look on David, though none but the two knew what was between them, and for David, he took it for a passing frenzy. But that he might have him out of his sight, the King gave him a high command in the army, so that David came seldom about the court. Yet his name was never out of Saul's ears. The very courtiers praised him, for Saul was too proud to show how it galled him, and all men thought him the King's favourite. More than all, Saul was afraid of David; his spirit crouched and became a fear before him: for the Lord was with David, and had departed from Saul.

Yet he could not bring himself to kill him. There was so much grace left in Saul. "It may be," he said to himself, "the Philistines will do that; let not my hand be upon him." For a long while he brooded. "Tell David," he said to his courtiers, "that he shall have my daughter to wife, and be the King's son-in-law, if he shall slay me a hundred Philistines for her marriage portion."

David went out, and came unwounded home, and instead of one hundred he had slain two hundred. The princess Michal was given him; well content, for she loved him. All men had a good word for the King's son-in-law; Jonathan was forever in his company. All things prospered in his hand, and Saul was still more afraid.

There came a day that he spoke openly to Jonathan, and Jonathan, amazed, pled with his father; spoke of the service David had given him; of the great day when he slew the Philistine, and no man in Israel so proud of him as Saul. As he listened, the day-light broke again upon Saul, and his heart turned again to David. Jonathan brought him to the presence, and for a while things were as they had been. Then came a great foray of the Philistines; David went to the war, and won great glory. But the day that he came victoriously home, the evil spirit came upon Saul. David, sent for to the presence, played on the harp before him; the King sat crouching, gripping his spear. But as he played, David saw the sudden gleam of hate in the King's face, and swerved, even as the javelin flashed through the air. When Saul came to himself, the room was empty, only for the javelin still quivering in the wall. This time, it woke no shame, but a greater fury. Messengers went hot foot to David's house to lie in wait and take him as he came out in the morning; but that night the princess, his wife, let him down through a window, and he fled.

It was some days after that a hunted man came to Jonathan by night; David, the King's son-in-law, harried like a runaway slave. "What have I done, Jonathan?" he asked him. "What is my sin before your father that he seeks my life?" "God forbid," said Jonathan, "it cannot be so, for there is nothing that my father keeps from me, and I have heard no word of it." "Your father knows that I have found grace in your sight," said David, "and he says, 'Let not Jonathan know this, lest he be grieved.' But truly, as the Lord liveth, and as thy soul liveth, there is but a step between me and death." They laid their plans together. The next day was the feast of the New Moon, and David would be gone; if Saul saw his place empty, and took it ill, it would be a sign that he meant evil. For three days David was to be hidden in the fields; and Jonathan would bring him word. "Now come," said Jonathan, "and let us go out into the field." They went out together: it was the dark of the moon, but they went in starlight. And there, standing face to face with David, Jonathan saw in the night the things that were to be. "David," he said, "the Lord shall be with thee, even as He once was with my father. Swear to me that when thy day is come, thou shalt show the kindness of God to me, if I be living, and to my children, if I be dead." They swore truth and loyalty to one another. Then Jonathan turned and came back to his house; and David lay under the stars.

The morrow was the feast of the New Moon. All the court was assembled; Saul came in, moody, and took his usual seat beside the wall; he had grown to hate an empty space behind him. Jonathan sat below him, Abner on Saul's other hand. David's place was empty. Saul eyed it as he sat down, but said nothing. The second day came; David's place was still empty. Saul turned abruptly to Jonathan.

"Why is it that the son of Jesse," he sneered as he said it, for he would not say his name, "comes not to the feast, yesterday nor to-day?"

"David asked three days' leave of me to go to Bethlehem, to his people," said Jonathan; "and I gave him leave. That is why he comes not to the King's table."

It was a lie, and Saul knew it. Something was brewing between his son, and the upstart who would take the kingdom from him. And as he looked at Jonathan, trying like a generous soul to shield him, the thought of the kingdom that he could never give him stabbed him; and his anguish broke in a spate of fury. "I tell you," he thundered, "you have chosen the son of Jesse to your own undoing, you, your mother's son. For as long as the son of Jesse lives upon the ground, there is safety neither for you, nor for your kingdom. So then, send for him and bring him to me, for he shall surely die."

Jonathan sat, giving his father look for look. "Why should he be slain?" he asked steadily. "What has he done?"

Saul flung his javelin. And Jonathan rose from the table in fierce anger, and did eat no meat that second day of the feast. For he was grieved for David, because his father had done him shame.

And in the morning, Jonathan went out into the field at the

time appointed with David, and took a little lad with him; for he had arranged with David what the sign was to be. And he said to the little lad, "Run, find out now the arrows which I shoot." And as the lad ran, he shot an arrow beyond him. And when the lad came to the place where the arrow had fallen, Jonathan cried out, "Is not the arrow beyond thee?" And David, hidden in the brushwood, heard, and knew that the King's heart had turned for ever from him. "Make speed," cried Jonathan, as though he cried to the boy. "Haste, stay not." But David still lay in the brushwood, for he longed to see Jonathan once again. The little lad gathered up the arrows, and brought them back to his master. Jonathan unslung his quiver. "Take them back," he said. "I will be after you in a little while." David heard the boy's steps crackling through the thicket, and in a little while silence. Jonathan stood waiting alone. Then David rose out of his hiding place to the south, and fell on his face before Jonathan. And they kissed one another and wept. And Jonathan said to David, "Go in peace, for we have sworn both of us in the name of the Lord, saying, The Lord be between me and thee, and between my seed and thy seed for ever."

Then David took leave of him, and took the road to the south, going into exile; and Jonathan turned and went into the city. And neither saw the other any more.

TEN

THE stillness of early morning lay on Nob, the city of the priests. It was a little town, on the road going south from Gibeah of Saul: for Jerusalem was not yet the Holy City, and the Ark of God was still in tents.

It was the morning of the Sabbath; Ahimelech the High Priest came out from the Holy Place, dropping the curtain of blue and purple and scarlet behind him. He was come from changing the shewbread, and the Holy Place was fragrant with the new loaves, and the fresh scattering of frankincense. Doeg the Edomite, the chief of Saul's herdsmen, watched the old priest through his half-closed eyes. Doeg was detained in the Temple courts that day, and the time hung heavy on his hands. The High Priest spoke to him mildly as he passed by. He did not like Doeg: he was red and grim like the cliffs of his own Edom, and Ahimelech wondered a little that the King should have an alien so high in his service. But he was a strong man of his hands, and no doubt the King knew his own business best. And since Doeg was there in the Temple court, there was surely some good thing in his heart towards God. The old man greeted him and passed on through the curtained doorway of the outer court, and across the sunlight to his own house.

The shadows were still long upon the ground. Out of them, at his own door, a man rose suddenly and faced him, dusty and travel-stained and sleepless-eyed. Ahimelech started back. Many a time had he seen David, the King's son-in-law; but never had he seen him like this.

"My son," he said, stammering in sudden fear, "why art thou alone, and no man with thee?"

All night David had lain in hiding, planning what he would

say. For he was hungry: for three days he had not tasted food, and he had no arms: both he must have, if he were to escape. Now he lied boldly.

"The King hath commanded me on business," he said, "and said unto me, 'Let no man know anything of this business whereon I send thee.' For my servants, they are to meet me at a certain place. Now, therefore, what is under thine hand? Give me five loaves to take with me, or whatever there is."

The old priest gazed at him, perplexed. "There is no bread ready," he said slowly, "but the shewbread, which is holy. But—"

"It is the King's business," said David, "and the bread is in a manner common. For is not the holy bread newly set upon the table?"

"Come then," said Ahimelech. Together they passed into the outer court, David walking with bent head, that no man might recognise him. Beside one of the posts he halted, his head sunk on his breast, while the High Priest, troubled and anxious, went alone into the Holy Place. In a little while he had come again, the sacred bread in his trembling hands. David, famished and eager, thrust it into his wallet, and lifted his head in quick relief. Across the sunlit court the eyes of Doeg the Edomite met his. Even so, in the old days, in the desert, had David come suddenly upon a snake.

For a moment Doeg's eyes held his. Then the Edomite's gaze went past him, as though he had seen nothing. David strung himself. "My father," he said to the priest, and his voice rang through the court, "is there not under thine hand spear or sword? For I have brought neither my sword nor my weapons with me, because the King's business required haste."

"There is no sword," said Ahimelech, "but the sword of Goliath of Gath: it is here in the Holy Place; wilt thou have that?"

"There is no sword like that," said David joyously. "Give it to me." The old man brought it out, bowed with the weight of it, and marvelling at the strength of this young man who girded it so lightly to his side. And as he turned and went bravely out, transfigured by the very touch of the hilt into the champion who had saved Israel, Ahimelech looked after him and blessed him. Once again, Doeg the Edomite lifted his eyes. David met him, look for look, and went proudly out. But as he went away, a nameless horror fell with the sunlight on the quiet streets, with the children at play. It was as though a hooded snake lay coiled on the altar stone. For himself—had be betrayed innocent blood?

It was months after that he knew. Word came to Saul that David, his enemy, was in the stronghold of Adullam, and with him four hundred men. So cruel had the fear become that the King now kept in the open, his spear in his hand, and his servants armed about him. He looked round on them, with hatred in his eyes—time-servers every one of them, following him for what they could get.

"What do you think you will get from the son of Jesse," he cried, "that you have every one conspired against me, and there is not one of you to shew me that my own son has made a league with the son of Jesse, and there is not one of you that is sorry for me, or will shew me that my own son has stirred up my servant against me, to lie in wait, as you see this day?"

His servants looked at one another. Where would the King's madness end? First David; then Jonathan; who next? Then Doeg the Edomite stepped forward.

"Sire," he said, "I saw the son of Jesse coming to Ahimelech, the priest, and Ahimelech gave him victuals and the sword of Goliath of Gath, and sent him on his way."

They sent for the High Priest, and for all the men of his house. And when they stood before the King, he raved upon them for traitors and conspirators, for that they had aided and abetted the son of Jesse to lie in wait for his life.

"Sire," answered the old priest, "and who is so faithful among all thy servants as David, who goeth at thy bidding, and is honourable in thine house? Let not the King impute evil to me or to my father's house. For indeed I knew nothing of all this, less or more."

But the evil thing that was in Saul had taken him wholly. No pity stirred in him for the good grey head bowed before him. They were against him, too, these priests: the priests and David and God, all in a league together. But he was King yet.

"Thou shalt surely die, Ahimelech," he said slowly, "thou and thy father's house." Then, turning to his men-at-arms, "Kill them," he cried, "the priests of the Lord: for their hand is with David too; for they knew when he fled, and would not shew it to me." The priests stood, eighty-five men, with the old High Priest at their head; clad in white, with no weapon in their hands, silent and unresisting. But fear fell on the men-at-arms. Not one dared lift his hand.

Saul glared round upon them, and his eyes met the eyes of Doeg the Edomite. "Thou," he said. And Doeg drew his sword.

Eighty-five men fell before the King's face that day. Then from Ramah Doeg went to Nob, the city of the priests. And when the sun rose, there was no living thing in its silent streets.

One man escaped, Abiathar, the High Priest's son. He came to David in his stronghold, and told him; and David, listening, knew what his lie had done. "I knew it that day," he cried, "when Doeg the Edomite was there, that he would surely tell Saul: I have occasioned the death of all the persons of thy father's house. Abide thou with me, fear not; for he that seeketh my life seeketh thy life; but with me thou shalt be in safeguard."

So Abiathar stayed with David, and in the end when David was come into his kingdom, Abiathar was High Priest in Jerusalem. But the night was grown darker about Saul.

ELEVEN

THERE was no hiding it now; the King's hate was an open hate. The story of the massacre at Nob ran through the land, and men wondered what the hate must be that had dared to strike for one man's sake the priests of God.

As for David, he haunted the hill slopes above the wilderness that goes down in great desolate stairs to the shore of the Dead Sea. He was a sort of Robin Hood; all the broken men in the country gathered to him; and there were many who were broken, for this new bitter Saul ruled with a high hand. They were good fighters; once, when the Philistines had come against a little border town, David and his men swooped down from the heights and drove them home again. But it was madness for David to trust himself inside four walls; Saul heard it, and came to take him in a trap, and the townsfolk would have betrayed him; but it was told to David, and he and his six hundred went out free.

Hunting David was like hunting a wild thing in a wood, and Saul's fury grew. Once when David was hiding in the woods south of the Wilderness of the Desolation, the men of the place brought word of it to Saul, and offered to betray him. But even they were staggered at the cry that broke from the King: "Blessed be ye of the Lord, for ye have had pity upon me." It was an ugly thing to hear from the man who once had the proudest heart in Israel. David was very near capture that time; Saul and his men were drawing a cordon round him. But news came of a Philistine raid, and the King drew off his army; when he came again, David was in the strongholds of Engedi, looking down on the Dead Sea.

Once again he came, and with him three thousand, to look for David in the rocks of the wild goats. David and his men were well hidden; they had found a cave with passages in the sides of it, and there they took shelter while the hunt went by. All day they heard the chase go on, and men shouting to one another on the rocks, while they lay close. The sounds had grown fainter; the chase was streaming down into the valley, when a shadow fell across the daylight at the mouth of the cave, and a man stooped his head to come in. The man beside David would have sprung, but David held him. He knew it for Saul the King.

He came a very little way into the cave, groping a little for the change from the sunlight blinded him. Suddenly the men realised that he had only come to rest himself a while in the shadow: that he did not know they were there. Back in the far recesses of the cave David's men came round him. "It has come true," they said, "what the Lord said to you has come true, that He would deliver your enemy into your hand. Go." If Saul had turned his head he might have seen the gleaming of the angry eyes, shining like wild cats' out of the dark. But he had no thought of danger; there was room in him for nothing but the hate that burned him like a slow fire.

Stepping lightly, David came up the cave, his knife in his hand. The men watched, craning forward. The King never stirred; his eyes were on the ground. David stooped, and they saw the gleam of the knife. Then he rose and came back to them, his face alight like a mischievous schoolboy, and a great fragment of Saul's robe in his hand. It was a joke after their own heart, and they forgave him the killing. But even as they chuckled, the light went out of David's face. "I should not have done it," he said. "God forbid that I should do so to my master, for he is the King." The men stared at him, taken aback; and even as they stared, Saul rose wearily and went slowly out. David's heart smote him, and he sprang forward.

Saul was not more than a few paces from the cave when he heard a voice behind him, saying, "My lord the King!" He turned and looked back, and there stood David, with a fragment of purple in his hand.

Saul stood gazing, and David bowed to the earth. Something stirred in Saul that would not let him cry out for his men to come and take him. He stood, and David began to speak.

"My lord," he said, "why do you listen to what men say to you, that David seeks to do you hurt? This day in the cave I could have killed you, and there were some with me who would gladly have killed you, but I would not." David saw the yearning in the face before him, that would so gladly believe it if it could. "See, my father," he urged, "I was near enough to cut off the skirt of your robe, but I killed you not. Yet you hunt my soul to take it. The Lord judge between us, and may He deliver me, for my hand will not be upon you."

Saul heard him. The voice broke through the tumult of evil noises that buzzed in his ear day and night, with a sound as kindly as the first crowing of a cock when one lies in the dark awake and afraid. The winds of the morning blew about him, and his heart broke for their sweetness. "Is it thy voice, O my dear son David?" he cried, and bowed his head on his hands and wept.

After a while he spoke. For a little while he saw clearly, and in the light of it he was the old generous Saul. "Thou art more righteous than I," he said. "Thou hast rewarded me good, and I rewarded thee evil. The Lord reward thee for the good thou didst to me this day. And I know—" Saul saw it face to face, the thing that poisoned his days, but for this once it had no power to sting him. "I know well that thou shalt surely be King. Swear to me, therefore, by the Lord, that thou wilt not cut off my name out of my father's house."

So David swore, and Saul turned and went slowly down the hill. He went in peace. For a moment he had seen the will of God concerning him, and he bowed himself before it. For in that moment he had seen it, not a naked sword stretched across the sky, but a river of still waters and green pastures, where a man might restore his soul.

> "For the face of God is a rock,
> But the face of the rock is fair."

TWELVE

SAMUEL was dead: and all Israel gathered to his burying. David alone dared not come: for Saul's brief tenderness towards him was already withered. Instead, he took the road with his men far south to the wilderness of Paran, where Ishmael had grown into a mighty hunter, hundreds of years before. For Saul, he heard of David's going, and took breath. The people noted that he was stricter than in Samuel's day, that he put down witchcraft with a high hand, like a man very zealous for the honour of God. Always in Saul's heart lingered the hope that God might yet be bought off.

Then one day the news came that David was back in his old haunts, the cliffs above the Wilderness of the Desolation. They came, the men of Ziph, sneaking into the King's presence with the offer to betray him. It was the very place where Saul had once taken his life from David's hand, but he forgot that. To purge Israel was good; but to get rid of one's rival was better and surer. Again Saul summoned his standing army, and came down to the wilderness, three thousand strong. They lay that night on the slopes of the Hill of Hachilah, and David's outposts brought in word that Saul was come.

That night three men left David's hold, and came through the brushwood to the heights above the camp. Below them the soldiers slept about their dying fires. The baggage was piled in a rampart like a ring; in the centre of it lay one mightier than any, his great spear thrust upright at his pillow. A light flickered into David's eyes. "Who will go down with me to Saul to the camp?" he asked joyously, and the younger of the men beside him said, "I."

Lightly they came down the face of the cliff, and through the sleeping ranks. Now and then, a soldier grunted in his sleep, but no one woke, for a deep sleep from God was upon them. In a little while David stood, and looked down at the face of the King. Not far from him lay Abner, old Abner, the captain of the host, not much changed since the days when David came to see the fight, a slip of a boy, with a cheese and newly-baked bread. Abishai touched David's sleeve. He too had been looking at the face of the King, but not as David looked.

"Let me smite him," he whispered, "smite him once with the spear to the earth, and I will not smite him the second time."

"God forbid," said David. "He is the King. The Lord shall smite him, or his day shall come to die, or he shall descend into battle and perish; but my hand shall not be upon him. Take the spear that is at his head, and the cruse of water, and let us go."

They took the great spear, thrust in the ground beside Saul's head, and the cruse of water that lay at his hand, and turned to go. Again they threaded their way through the sleeping men, passed the rampart of the baggage, and across the valley to the rising ground. There they stood and looked back, marvelling a little that men should sleep so sound, the enemy so near, and know it not. Then David threw back his head.

"Answerest thou not, Abner?" he cried, and the clear call scattered the drowsiness that lay on Abner's brain. The old chief struggled upright.

"Who art thou that criest to the King?" he shouted stormily.

"Art thou not a valiant man?" the gay voice went on, mocking out of the darkness. "Who is like unto thee in Israel, O Abner, captain of the host? Why then didst thou not keep thy lord the King? There came in one even now to destroy him. And now, see where the King's spear is, and the cruse of water that was at his pillow."

The whole camp was awake: Abner, fuming and wrathful, struggled with the fastenings of his armour. But it was for another than Abner that David spoke, and another than Abner an-

swered him. David far off on the hill, could see the gigantic figure of Saul, upright, and straining, his hand over his eyes, into
the darkness beyond the fires.

"Is this thy voice, my son David?" he asked, with that strange
simplicity that made his least word great.

"It is my voice, my lord, O King."

There fell a silence. Then with one last effort David set himself to banish for ever the evil mist that clogged the King's brain.

"My lord," he said earnestly, "hear. What have I done? If this
evil imagining is from the Lord, make peace with Him; but if
it be men who have stirred thee up against me, let them be ac-
cursed, for they have driven me out of the inheritance of God.
Let not my blood fall to the earth, for the King of Israel is come
out as when one doth hunt a partridge in the mountains."

Then said Saul, "I have sinned; come back, my son David, for
I will no more do thee harm, because my soul was precious in
thine eyes this day. Behold, I have played the fool, and have
erred exceedingly."

For a moment David stood irresolute. To go back, and take
the King at his word; to company with him day and night, and
fight for him with the evil spirit that was destroying him; it was
too great a risk.

"My lord," he said, "send one of thy young men to fetch thy
spear. And may my life be as dear in the sight of God, as thy
life was in mine this day."

He was not coming back. Saul knew it and once again he saw
upon the night the things that were to be. Standing there, he
lifted his hand and blessed him. "Blessed be thou, my son
David," he said. "Thou shalt do great things, and thou shalt still
prevail."

David turned on the brow of the hill and looked back. Saul
still stood, gazing into the night, his hand upraised in blessing.
It was David's last sight of Saul the King.

THIRTEEN

THEY had parted, David and Saul; Saul to his own place, but David to the King of the Philistines; for he said there was no safety for him in the coasts of Israel. Saul heard that he was in Gath, Goliath's city, and he sought for him no more. And then the Philistines declared war on Israel.

It was a great muster, the greatest since their route in the Valley of the Terebinth, when Goliath was slain. Then, they had attacked from the south; now it was from the north; Saul was to be very near the hills of his first campaign. The Philistines encamped on Little Hermon, with the village of Shunem below them, that rich little village where one of the prophets came long afterwards, and brought a little child to life who was stricken in the harvest fields. Behind them to the north was a valley, and on its other side the dreary mountain slope on which Endor lay; before them to the south a plain, stretching to the foot of Mount Gilboa, where Saul encamped with his men.

Day after day Saul watched the hosts of the Philistines gathering, and he was sore afraid. He sought a sign from God in a dream, but no dream came. He bade the prophets enquire of God for him, but they said that there was no answer. Once, Samuel had told him what to do, and he had not done it, and Samuel was dead. Then said Saul to his servants, "Seek me out a woman that hath a familiar spirit, and I will enquire of her." Samuel had said that rebellion was as the sin of witchcraft. Then this sin also would be his, but an answer he would have.

They told him that there was a woman who had a familiar spirit at Endor. It was eight miles to Endor, round the eastern spur of the ridge where the Philistines lay, among the dark hills behind them. Saul disguised himself that none might know it was the King, and went, and two men with him, and came to the woman by night. And he said, "I pray thee, divine unto me by thy familiar spirit, and bring me up him whom I shall name unto thee."

And the woman said unto him, "Thou knowest what Saul hath done, that he hath put to death every one that hath a familiar spirit; why dost thou lay a snare for my life?" Then Saul sware unto her, "As the Lord liveth, there shall no punishment happen to thee for this thing." Then said the woman, "Whom shall I bring up unto thee?" And he said, "Samuel."

When the woman saw Samuel—but the King saw him not—she cried with a great cry: and she said to Saul, "Why hast thou deceived me? For thou art Saul." "Be not afraid," said the King; "what sawest thou?" And the woman said, "I saw a god ascending out of the earth." Then said the King, "What form is he of?" And she said, "An old man cometh up, and he is covered with a mantle." Then Saul knew that it was Samuel, and he knelt with his face to the ground.

And Samuel said to Saul, "Why hast thou disquieted me to bring me up?" And Saul answered, "I am sore distressed. For the Philistines make war against me, and God is departed from me, and answereth me no more: therefore I have called thee, that thou mayest make known unto me what I shall do."

Then said Samuel, "Why dost thou ask of me, seeing the Lord is departed from thee, and is become thine enemy? The Lord hath done as He said; He hath rent the kingdom out of thy hand, and given it to thy neighbour, to David. Because thou didst not obey the voice of the Lord, therefore the Lord doeth this thing unto thee this day. Moreover, the Lord will deliver Israel with thee into the hand of the Philistines: and to-morrow shalt thou and thy sons be with me: and the Lord shall also deliver the host of Israel into the hand of the Philistines."

Then Saul fell straightway all his length upon the ground.

After a time the woman came and found him: and there was no strength in him, for he had eaten no bread all the day, nor all the night.

"My lord," she said, "I put my life in my hand, and hearkened to thy words. Now then, I pray thee, hearken to my words, and let me set a morsel of bread before thee; and eat, that thou mayest have strength when thou goest on thy way." But he refused, and said, "I will not eat."

They came to him, then, his two servants, and the woman, and entreated him. And he listened to them, and rose from the earth, and sat on the bed. The woman made haste, and in a little while the house was filled with the smell of roasting meat, and the warmth of the baking of bread; and Saul's servants spoke to one another in low voices, and to the woman as she came and went about the fire. And Saul sat on the bed, and life went about him with all its remembered sounds and noises, and he saw it at an end for him.

It was still night when their meal was ended, and they rose up and went their way, journeying in the chill before the dawn. Saul made no moan. Once at the beginning, when he stood on the threshold of his kingdom, he had said no word; now at the end, in the moment of his utter defeat, he held his peace.

The camp was still asleep as he passed through it to his tent; and when at dawn the trumpets of the Philistines blew upon the heights, he came from it to marshal his men.

It was the Philistines who attacked. All day the oncoming tide surged and ebbed, and surged again a little higher on the mountain slope; for the men of Israel fled before the Philistines, and fell down slain on Mount Gilboa. But it was on one man that the fury of the battle centred, the man who had kept them at bay for forty years; the Philistines followed hard on Saul and his sons. Jonathan was the first to fall; then Abinadab; then Melchishuah; and Saul was left alone. One man saw him towards the end of the fight, saw him sore wounded and leaning on his spear, and knew he would not live after he had fallen. But the day wore to evening and Saul was yet alive. They dared not come near him to single combat; it is ill for the young lions to face the old one dying. But the archers far off marked him, and the arrows fell thick, and still they crept nearer.

Then said Saul to his armour-bearer, "Draw thy sword, and thrust me through, lest these uncircumcised come and abuse me." But the armour-bearer would not, because he was Saul the King. Then Saul took his own sword, and fell upon it; and when his armour-bearer saw that Saul was dead, he fell likewise upon his sword and died with him. So Saul died, and his three sons, and his armour-bearer, and all his men, that same day together.

On the morrow, when the Philistines came to strip the slain, they found Saul and his three sons fallen in Mount Gilboa. His head they took, and hung it in the temple of Dagon their god; and his armour in the temple of their goddess Ashtaroth; but his body they hung on the walls of Beth-shan. From all the little villages the people fled, to the other side of Jordan, and into their desolate houses the Philistines came, and lived there.

But when the men of Jabesh-Gilead heard what they had done to Saul, they remembered the great deliverance he had wrought for them in the days of his youth. And all the valiant men arose and went all night and took the body of Saul and the bodies of his sons from the walls of Beth-shan; and by that road which Saul had taken at the head of a great host, they carried his body to burial; and they mourned for him with a great mourning.

✻ ✻ ✻ ✻ ✻

So this was the end of the story of Saul the King; an uncrowned head on a spike in the house of the fish-bellied god; a suit of armour rusting in the temple of Ashtaroth; a little dust at the root of the Gilead oaks; and a name in the greatest dirge that ever was sung for the dead. Yet was God very merciful to him in his death. For it was his own sword that took the kingdom from him, the kingdom that had come between him and God; and that long quarrel ended, there was nothing between them any more. So he passed over; and the God who was not found of Saul the King stood waiting to be found of Saul the man.

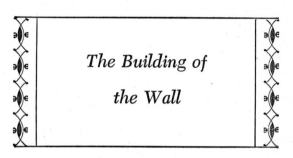

The Building of

the Wall

ONE

NEHEMIAH, the King's cupbearer, sat and talked with his brother in Shushan, which was the winter palace of the Persian Kings. They called it Shushan, because in April the fields were white with lilies, and there were great beds of lilies in the river. It was a country of rivers, and the one that washed the walls of the palace flowed over sands so golden that afterwards there was a legend that only the sons of the Kings might drink of it. It was December, but in Shushan it was not cold. Not so cold as it had been coming from the fords of the Euphrates across the Mesopotamian plains. The man with whom Nehemiah talked was fresh from that journey, and he said it was bitter. It was clear autumn weather when he left Jerusalem, he went on; but he had rued the journey many times before he was at the end of it.

Nehemiah looked at his brother, and there was envy in his eyes. "I would give a good deal," he said, "that for one year you were the King's cupbearer, and not I."

"Why?" said Hanani.

"The King will not let me out of his sight. If it were not for that, it is not the snow on the passes that would keep me from Jerusalem."

"And I would give as much," said his brother, "that I had never seen it."

"Man," said Nehemiah, "what ails you? You went to Jerusalem as light as an arrow, and you are home from it sick and sullen, and will not name its name. And you have told me of the roads and the fords, and the gardens of Damascus, but never a word of the place you would have given your eyes to see."

For a while Hanani sat, watching the quiet flowing of the river.

"Do you remember," he said suddenly, "what they sang us to sleep with when we were children—

> 'By the rivers of Babylon we sat and wept,
> Remembering thee.
> If I forget thee, O Jerusalem—' "

"They sing it yet," said Nehemiah.

"Do you remember the day they took us to see the Hanging Gardens of Semiramis? and we came back full of it and our mother said, 'Ah, but if you saw the King's Gardens in Jerusalem, down in the valley where the rivers meet!' And the day we came back boasting about the walls of Babylon and how high they were, and the hundred gates in them, and she made us learn the gates in Jerusalem, and drew a picture on the sand—the Fish Gate and the Fountain Gate, the Valley Gate—do you remember her telling us about the Dragon Well?—and the City Gate—are they there still, Hanani?"

"Still?" said Hanani. "Man, the wall is level with the ground, and the gates are burned with fire."

Nehemiah looked at him, dumb.

"I tell you," said Hanani, "I saw the blackened stumps of them; and I saw a fox go into its earth where she said the Tower of the Furnace would be. There is a landslide at the Gate of the Fountain, and the Pool is choked. Do you remember how she used to say, 'The Waters of Shiloh that go softly, that go softly'?"

Nehemiah nodded.

" 'Beautiful for situation, the joy of the whole earth.' If you saw it! A rubble of houses on a ridge of rock, with a trickle of water through it half-dry in the heat, bleached like the ribs of a thing dead in the desert."

"Have done," said Nehemiah. "It is the city of God."

Hanani moved to the window and stood looking out.

"Bel has a finer temple in Babylon than He has yonder in Jerusalem," he said bitterly. "They say that when they laid the foundation of it the old men who had seen the first House took up a wail for the glory of it, and the rest of them shouting for joy, so that you could not have told the voice of the shouting for the voice of the weeping."

Nehemiah lifted his head. " 'The glory of this latter house shall be greater than that of the former,' " he quoted, " 'and in this place will I give peace.' "

"It is long of coming," said Hanani. "It is ninety years since they went out from Babylon, 'with everlasting joy upon their heads,' and the place is a wilderness yet. Blight and mildew and locusts and bad harvests—there is no heart left in them. And the loneliness of it—there is a prophet among them that says the day will come when the streets of the city will be full of boys and girls playing in the streets of it. They are empty enough now, and the owls and bats are nesting in the tombs of the Kings. Our own graves—the graves of our fathers—"

He turned and went out. Nehemiah watched him go, with eyes that did not see him. They saw the mountain of Zion desolate, the foxes walk upon it. Then a great weeping took him, and as he wept he cried on the name of God: "O Lord God of heaven, the great and terrible God."

TWO

WHEN Nehemiah was little, every night in the sunset, beyond the walls of Babylon, he saw Jerusalem. Sometimes the sun went down over the plains in one great sapphire sea, with no clouds to wait upon it. Nehemiah did not care for those nights. But sometimes it went down behind great mountains of cloud, with turrets on the ridge of them that glowed with edges of fire. He saw them from his bed before he went to sleep, and as he watched them his mother crooned above his bed.

"If I forget thee, O Jerusalem!"

For a long time Nehemiah believed that that city of fire was Jerusalem, so far off to the west that one could only see it when the sun went down behind it. He never said it to anyone; and when he grew older he found out for himself that it was not true: that Jerusalem was so far away that only the sun himself could see it from Babylon. But it was still a fairy city to him; and still as the sun went down over the edge of the world he would think to himself, "It is shining red on Jerusalem, and red on the pool in the King's Garden, and the boughs of the olive trees are red, standing over it."

He knew that it was a city on a rock; he made his mother tell him over and over again how it first was taken: how David and his men crept up the stony water-course under the walls, dry in the heat, so that a man could slip through, and were inside before the men peering on the walls had seen what they were about; and so it was called the City of David. All the same he thought of it as a place of streams, with a river flowing through it, the river in the Psalms, "whose streams make glad the city of God." And when he walked in the level fields round Babylon, and saw the endless little canals with their silent sleeping water, he pictured to himself steep little brooks in the streets of Jerusalem, and the sound of falling water always in one's ears. There were no mountains about Babylon, only the great masonry of the walls: and the verse he liked best in the Psalms was the one that begins, "As the mountains are round about Jerusalem."

There was another story that he never tired of hearing, and yet he hated it, for it left him shaken and afraid: how Nebuchadnezzar, King of Babylon, came marching with all his army, and sat down before Jerusalem to a siege. For a year and a half the siege went on, and children and grown men died of hunger in the streets; and Jeremiah the prophet walked the city day and night crying to the people to surrender and go out to the Chaldeans, for that God would fight for them no more. And the princes were angry, and they took Jeremiah and put him in a dungeon so deep that they had to let him down with cords; there was no water in the dungeon, but mire, and Jeremiah sank in the mire. But the King, Zedekiah, could not rest for the words that he had said, and he sent men to the dungeon and they threw down rags to Jeremiah to put under his armpits, that the cords might not hurt him, and they pulled him up and left him in the court of the prison. Then the King came himself by stealth and said to Jeremiah, "What shall I do?" And Jeremiah said, "Obey the voice of the Lord, and go out to the princes of Babylon, and your soul shall live, and the city shall be saved; but if you refuse to go, you shall see your wives and your children brought out to the Chaldeans, and yourself shall be taken by the hand of the King of Babylon; and you shall cause this city to be burned with fire." Then Zedekiah went from him, and he was very sore afraid. But he feared lest the princes should despise him for a coward, and so he did not surrender.

July came, and the city was stifling hot, and the brooks were dry. In five more nights the moon would be at the full. And on the ninth night, at midnight the wall was breached, and the princes of Babylon came in and sat in the middle gate, and the torches flared before them. Zedekiah saw them, and his men of war, and they fled, down through the olives of the King's Garden, and out through the gate between the two walls, and on to the way of the plain. But the Chaldeans went after them, and overtook them in the plains of Jericho, and brought Zedekiah bound before their King. And Nebuchadnezzar slew his two sons before his eyes, and brought him in chains to Babylon. And the Kings of Babylon drank their wine from the sacred cups of the Temple and praised the gods that were gods of gold and silver and wood and stone.

"What did God do it for?" Nehemiah had asked once in great anger. And his mother repeated to him the words she had learned from her mother, words that went like a chant:

"The Lord God of their fathers sent to them by His messengers, rising up early and sending; because He had compassion on His people and His dwelling place: but they mocked the messengers of God and despised His words and misused His prophets, until the wrath of the Lord rose against His people, till there was no remedy. Therefore He brought upon them the King of the Chaldeans, who slew their young men with the sword in the house of their sanctuary, and had no compassion upon young man or maiden, old man or him that stooped for age. And all the vessels of the house of God, and the treasures of the King, and of his princes, all these he brought to Babylon. And they burnt the house of God, and broke down the wall of Jerusalem, and burnt all the palaces thereof with fire. And them that had escaped from the sword carried he away to Babylon where they were servants to him and his sons until the reign of the kingdom of Persia; and the land lay desolate and kept sabbath, to fulfil the seventy years."

It was an old story now; it had been old even when Nehemiah heard it first. Long before he was born God had had pity on His people. Babylon had fallen, and their new masters, the Persian

Kings, were merciful, and had let them, as many as would, go back. They had even sent back the sacred cups of the Temple and its treasures. The new Temple was built; had been standing it would soon be a hundred years. Yet a blight was still upon the city, and its streets were still forlorn. What ailed it? Could it be that God's anger was not yet turned away, and His hand was stretched out still?

THREE

THEN Nehemiah fell on his knees and prayed. For he saw the wrath of God brooding over the ruined city on the rock like a cloud big with thunder; but as he prayed it seemed to him that he saw above the cloud, and the sun shone on it, and the cloud was white and soft like the breast of a dove. And the prayer that had begun with the name of the great and terrible God changed into a cry to a God that kept covenant and mercy. They passed before Nehemiah's eyes, the generations that had played and grown old and died in the streets of Jerusalem, their hardness to one another, and their strange gods, and the drunkenness of their feasts; it seemed to him that he was with them, and their sins were his sins, and he lifted them up in his hands to the mercy of God. He saw the cloud hang lower over Jerusalem, and lightning break forth from it and scorch her palaces, and the smoke of a great burning; and then along the eastern road he saw the captives go, bound and driven, into a strange land, and the cry of footsore men was in his ears. Then the roads were empty and the city desolate, and over all the land the brooding thunderous light. And then he saw them coming back, in twos and threes, from the uttermost part of heaven, for so the old words ran, and the great cloud was rent here and there, and the light fell through like silver rain. A little more, and it would break and scatter into soft white flakes, and drift into the unfathomable blue above the sea. Even as Nehemiah prayed he saw it break: and he knew what he must do. For there was one man under God who held Jerusalem in the hollow of his hand, and that man was his master, Artaxerxes, the King.

It was in December that Nehemiah saw these things. It was April, the month of the Green Ears in Palestine, before his moment came. The moon was at the full, and Nehemiah, standing behind the King at the banquet, gazed through the pillars into the shining night, and the warm air blew upon his face. Spring came early in Shushan, and the frogs in the lily beds by the river were loud. In Jerusalem they would be keeping the Passover; and the same moon rode over the palace at Shushan, and the huddle of dim houses on the rock. In Jerusalem they broke the unleavened bread and ate the bitter herbs of longing; and he stood in purple and poured the wine, with the savour of rich meats in his nostrils and the fragrance of musk: for the Queen sat by her husband that night, and when she stirred she breathed perfume like a flower. Somewhere in Jerusalem the moon was shining cold on the stones of what was a king's house once; there would be black shadows of cypress on the untended graves. The cup at the King's right hand was empty; Nehemiah stooped to pour the wine, and the King, glancing up, saw the misery in his eyes.

"Art sick, man?" he asked kindly: he liked Nehemiah, and it struck him that he, who was such a good fellow, had had little to say that night.

"I am not sick," said Nehemiah.

"Then," said the King, "why is thy countenance sad?" His own face clouded. His hand was outstretched to the wine-cup, but he drew it back again, with a sudden quick suspicion. Poison was never far from the Persian Kings.

"This is nothing else," he said grimly, "but evil of heart."

Then Nehemiah was very sore afraid.

"O King," he cried, "live for ever!" He hesitated, and then the words came in spate. "Why should not my countenance be sad, when the city, the place of my fathers' sepulchres, lieth waste, and the gates thereof burned with fire?"

The words rang through the banqueting hall like a cry. It was poetry he was speaking, not the common speech of men. It fell on the King's ear like a fragment of the chant that all Babylon heard from the slave-gangs on the roads. He gazed at Nehemiah, perplexed. Rich—he knew him to be rich, and his father before him; famous and envied, for to be the King's cupbearer was a thing the Persian nobles would sell their souls for: what had come upon the man that his easy pleasant speech had gone from him, and he had broken into a cry like that? But there was magic in it; and though the King had never seen Jerusalem, he saw for a moment what Nehemiah saw. The man before him was a strange man to him; the Persian courtier was gone, and in his stead the dreamer of dreams that was in every Hebrew, that made them for all time the men from Beyond the River.

"What is it," said the King slowly, "that you would ask me?" Nehemiah's sudden outburst was spent; he marvelled at himself. But he had spoken better than he knew. For a moment he called to mind the King who watched above Jerusalem and Shushan alike; and then he knelt before the lesser King.

"If it please the King," he said, "and if thy servant have found favour in thy sight, that thou wouldst send me unto Judah, unto the city of my fathers' sepulchres, that I may build it."

The King sat with his chin in his hands, frowning. He liked Nehemiah: he all but loved him: he was the one man in all his court in whom he believed with his whole heart. He could not let him go. The Queen beside him stirred, and the King, looking at her, saw her eyes very pitiful. For to be a queen in Persia was also to be a captive; and the cry in the cupbearer's voice had stirred the old pain. She did not speak, but her eyes said, "Let him go."

"How long would you want to be away?" asked the King, irritably. "When will you come back?"

Then Nehemiah knew that he had his request. "It pleased the King to send me," he wrote in his journal, "and I set him a time." Letters also he asked, to the governors beyond the river, for safe conduct until he came into Judah; a letter also—for Nehemiah forgot nothing—to Asaph, the keeper of the King's forest, to give timber to make beams for the gates of the palace that once was Solomon's, and for the city gates, and for what was to be his own house in Jerusalem. "And the King granted me," he wrote, "according to the good hand of my God upon me." So with that good hand upon him, Nehemiah set out for Jerusalem.

FOUR

So," wrote Nehemiah in his journal, "I came to Jerusalem." He noted down his escort of captains and horsemen: and how the governors beyond the river received his passports from the King. Also as he came down through Samaria he had an interview with Sanballat, the governor, and saw the scowl on his face behind all his politeness, and the dark face of Tobiah the servant, where he stood behind his chair. Nehemiah made a note of them, that they would do all the mischief they could, and went his way.

The road had been climbing up for a long time under the shelter of the olives: Nehemiah was glad of the shade, for they had ridden hard that day, knowing that they were near the end of their journey. Just before him the road turned sharply round the spur of the hill, the guide in front slackened his jog trot and stood still, pointing with his hand. Nehemiah rode up to him and saw Jerusalem across the valley. He drew rein and sat his horse, gazing. The horsemen behind him halted.

There it was, Jerusalem, the joy of the whole earth: it clung to the rock on which it was built, like a cluster of shabby swallows' nests: so small, so poor, so utterly forlorn, that the sight of it struck at his heart. The afternoon sun blazed down upon it, and the little city slept in its dust like a stray dog sleeping on the road. It looked masterless, as if no one cared for its soul.

Even as Nehemiah gazed, something stirred. The small figure of a runner dashed up to the parched road, and in through the gap in the mound that had once been the city gates. There seemed to be no small commotion inside: white figures came and stood gazing, their hands over their eyes: presently they formed in procession, and came soberly down the road into the valley.

Nehemiah guessed that it was a deputation of the chief men of the city come out to meet the new governor, and he set his horse in motion. They had not looked for him before sundown, for Nehemiah in his eagerness had shortened the halt at noon: some of them were barely wakened from their afternoon sleep. Very courteous they were: but curiously lack-lustre. They seemed in no way gratified that the new governor was a man of their own race. It seemed to Nehemiah that they spoke to him, and he answered them, like people moving and talking in their sleep. They climbed the hill slowly. Nehemiah looked neither to the right hand nor to the left. Only as he neared the gap he saw a fragment of the gatepost sticking up, black and charred, and convolvulus creeping over the fallen stones. The elder who held his bridle, and walked at his horse's head, was still making ex-cuse that they had not met him sooner, and Nehemiah heard, and heard not.

A scrap of a verse that they used to sing in Babylon was ringing in his ears:

> "I was glad when they said unto me,
> Let us go into the house of the Lord,
> Our feet shall stand within thy gates,
> O Jerusalem."

It had come true for him, but he rode through the gate with a dull weight at his heart.

There were not many in the streets. Nehemiah, used to the thronging crowds in Babylon, found them strangely empty. The few who were stirring made obeisance to the new governor; but they gazed at him with no expectation in their eyes. It was a lifeless afternoon: it seemed to him, as he rode, that no wind had blown for a long time in the streets: and no wind in the people's hearts. They seemed poor. The elders who had met him were rich. There was a sort of dull magnificence about them. But these in the streets were shabby and lean. Once an old man ran before him crying out that his daughter was sold for a slave, and pointing to the venerable old man at his horse's head, but the guards hustled him aside, and Nehemiah turning his head, saw him throwing dust in the air, and crying curses. He said nothing, but he pondered it in his mind, promising himself that the elder should hear of it again. Meantime he was his host, for the governor's house was not yet built.

For three days Nehemiah hardly left the house. There was much business to be done, and many headmen from the villages came to pay their respects. Once he went to the Temple, and set his mouth when he saw the meanness of the service, and the ignorance of the priests. They hung about the courts, gossiping with the idlers. A man came up the steps, bringing a sheep to sacrifice, and it limped as it came. They brought God what was of little use to themselves. And yet his heart was sore for them. Could they respect any, when they had no respect for themselves? They were citizens of a mean city. They had not what the poorest hamlet in the hills had a right to, its own wall.

FIVE

ALL this time Nehemiah said nothing of what was in his heart. But with the passing of the crowded empty days the craving grew in him to see Jerusalem, his city, for himself. Always the elders were at his elbow, pointing to this and that. Sometimes he wondered at himself. Never had he seemed so far away from it, as now that he walked in its streets.

It was the evening of the third day: there had been a feast at the house of the high priest, and Nehemiah had come from it, utterly weary. The house was asleep: Nehemiah sat brooding, watching the moon swing slowly up over the valley of Hinnom: the gorge was very black. Suddenly he knew what he must do. Rising, he called for his own servants; in a few moments his horse was saddled, and led quietly through the archway of the court into the moonlit street. There he mounted, his men following him.

Down through the sleeping streets he rode, and out by the Valley Gate. Over against him was the Dragon Well. He got down from his horse and for the sake of the boy that had been Nehemiah, flung a pebble into the echoing blackness, waiting with his hand on the mossy parapet for the little tinkling splash that came up to him from far below. Then he mounted, and rode slowly down the valley, slowly, for the ground was rough, and fragments of the wall lay in tumbled heaps. Thistles grew here and there, and the swollen bulk of cactus looked blue and ugly in the moonlight. In the shadow of the ruins the nettles grew tall, and the faint dank smell of them was in the air. It was an evil place.

All down the valley of Hinnom he rode. Then the wall turned north at the gate where they carried out the refuse and flung it into the valley: that was what made it so foul. He was skirting the edge of the valley of the Kedron; he could hear the brook below him in the darkness, trickling over the stones. Soon he should come to the Fountain Gate and the King's Pool. For he knew the King's Garden must be close by: he had not asked about it since he came: he wanted—for the sake of the boy Nehemiah—to see it by himself. Already he was looking for the gap when the horse stumbled under him, all but to his knees. There had been a landslide; the wall falling had taken the earth with it, and the ground fell away to the gorge in a great scar of loose earth and huge stones. Nehemiah left his horse, and scrambled on foot.

Somewhere to the left a solitary frog was croaking: would it be at the King's Pool? He turned and made his way through a tangle of briars, stooping now and then under the straggling branches of neglected apple trees. Once he stumbled on a bed of wild thyme, and for a moment all the sweetness of forgotten summer nights in the King's Garden was in its pungent breath. The frog had stopped his croaking, but the moon showed him the King's Pool: it was choked with rubbish, and green scum was on the water. Back to the valley he came, and guiding himself by the sound of the brook and the broken outline of the ramparts, he clambered along the slope.

For a long time he went blindly on. Then he stopped, and gazed at the jagged line stretching to the north. He had come out to see his city: had he not seen enough? He turned, and came to where his servants waited with his horse, mounted and rode back to the Valley Gate. Jerusalem was a broken thing: the city of his dreams was fallen. Then, please God, HE WOULD BEGIN TO BUILD IT NEW TO-MORROW.

SIX

NEHEMIAH sat on the flat roof of the house where he was lodging till the governor's house should be built. He was writing in his journal, but every now and then he got up and walked to the parapet and looked down; and even when he went back his hand would lie idle on the page, and he would sit listening, well pleased. Fourteen days ago he had sat here in the dusk and watched the moon rise over the silent valley; there was no sound then but the barking of a fox somewhere in its shadow. Now the clinking of trowels was in the air, and the cheerful din of many men all working together. When he walked to the parapet and looked down, the valley below him swarmed like an ant-hill, and already the broad even line of masonry was showing white in the twilight.

"I said to them," wrote Nehemiah, " 'Ye see the distress that we are in, how Jerusalem lieth waste, and the gates thereof are burned with fire; come and let us build up the wall, that we be no more a reproach.' Then I told them of the good hand of my God upon me, and also the King's words that he had spoken unto me. And they said, 'Let us rise up and build.' So they strengthened their hands for the good work.

"Then the high priest rose up with his brethren the priests and builded the Sheep Gate, and the wall as far as the Tower of Hananeel—indeed they did well, the priests," said Nehemiah to himself, "and I think better of them than when I came—and next unto them builded the men of Jericho . . . and next unto them the men of Tekoa repaired. They did well, the men of Tekoa, and it is a backward, poor place too. But their nobles did not put their necks to it. I will write that down," said Nehemiah, "for it is not fair that they should get the credit of it—and the Old Gate—there were two men repaired the Old Gate—"

Nehemiah stopped to look up the names in the tablets that swung at his girdle, and an indignant howl rose from the courtyard below him. The governor crossed to the inner parapet and looked down. The voice that howled was the voice of Elizabeth, who was five; and already the governor was a friend of Elizabeth's. Elizabeth had been building her little wall of Jerusalem in the courtyard all day, and as the governor came and went he stopped to admire the line of it, or to advise her that her mortar was too wet. But Shammai, who was seven, had just come back with his father from the real wall; and he had scoffed at Elizabeth's, and demanded his trowel, and said that girls were no good and wouldn't be allowed to touch the wall that they were all building for the Tirshatha. Only men could do that, and boys like him. He had carried mortar for two hours that afternoon. It was at this point that Elizabeth howled.

"Ask the Tirshatha!" said Shammai triumphantly.

"What is it, Elizabeth?" said the voice of the Tirshatha high above their heads. The two peered up at him. Elizabeth's wail ceased, and she pointed a muddy finger at her brother.

"It is not true, Tirshatha, what Shammai said?"

"What did you say, Shammai?"

"I said it was my trowel," said Shammai, prodding his bare toe into Elizabeth's mortar. "And it is my trowel."

"It was not that," said Elizabeth, furious. "He said they wouldn't let a woman touch the wall they are building for you. Sure it is not true, Tirshatha?"

"It is not true. Listen to this, Shammai." The Tirshatha was turning over his tablets. "'After the Tower of the Furnaces repaired Shallum, the ruler of the half part of Jerusalem, he and his daughters.' I passed that way to-day, and there was not a man on the wall working better."

"Is that written down?" said Shammai suspiciously.

"It is written down, and the roll will be kept in the Temple for ever."

Shammai humped himself and straggled towards the house. Elizabeth stood gazing at the dim figure of the Tirshatha against the twilight sky.

"Then could I build the wall for you to-morrow?" said Elizabeth.

"You and I will build a piece together," said the Tirshatha. "But it is not for me they are building it, Elizabeth."

"Who for?" said Elizabeth.

"Jehovah," said the Tirshatha. "Listen, Elizabeth." The darkness had fallen, and the men were leaving the wall for the night. They were singing as they went.

> "Except the Lord do build the house,
> The builders lose their pain.
> Except the Lord the city keep,
> The watchmen watch in vain.

> " 'Tis vain for you to rise betimes;
> Or late from rest to keep,
> To feed on sorrow's bread: so gives
> He his beloved sleep."

"It is a good verse to go to bed on," said the Tirshatha. "Goodnight, Elizabeth." Elizabeth trotted in. The Tirshatha collected his parchments and went down the steps, to finish his journal by lamplight.

SEVEN

NEHEMIAH was taking a visitor round the walls. He was a countryman of his own, a Jew, but he lived on the border, and knew as much of Samaria as he did of Judaea. It was his first visit to Jerusalem since the wall began to be built: but he had written to Nehemiah and sent presents towards the building. Now that he had come himself, the Tirshatha was well pleased to see him. He was very silent as Nehemiah took him round. Even when Nehemiah dragged him up a great rubbish heap that he might see the long sweep of the foundations above the Kedron, he had not a word to say. Nehemiah stood looking at it, and his pride in it fell a little. Always he had seen the wall, not as it was, but as it was going to be. Now that he saw it through a strange man's eyes, he wondered if it was so great a matter after all. They were not practised masons, of course: bits of wall had had to be built over again: the whole looked shabby, even a little patchy.

"Of course," said Nehemiah, "there is a good deal to be done yet."

"There is," said the visitor heavily.

Nehemiah turned and looked at him. "What ails you, man?" he asked. The man from the border turned suddenly away. "I had not meant to tell you," he broke out, "but it is burning me. It was Sanballat the governor, and that ill-looked Tobiah the Ammonite that is his servant. They were holding a review of the troops, and Sanballat said before all the men, 'Have you heard of the doings of these feeble Jews? It is fortifying themselves they are—with a wall to be built in a day, as soon as they have looked out stones enough from the rubbish of the old one that was burned.' And Tobiah the Ammonite said, 'They made a great day's building, I am hearing, and in the night a fox walked on it, and their wall came down about his heels.' And then they all fell to laughing."

Nehemiah did not say much. That night he wrote it all down in his journal, and sat and looked at it. It was very bitter. "O God," he wrote, "we are despised." It was the first time Nehemiah had been laughed at, and he was a proud man. Was this what he had come from Babylon for, to make a fool of himself, and be laughed at by a half-caste? In Babylon, Sanballat would have come to the King's cupbearer with presents. If he had wanted a favour, he would have crawled to him. Nehemiah set his mouth. The next morning as he went round the wall he dropped a word here and there. In their fury the men worked like giants, and in a day or two the circuit of the wall was joined. "Now they may laugh," said Nehemiah.

But this time they did not laugh. In a few days there came rumours from Samaria that Sanballat and Tobiah the Ammonite were plotting. Nehemiah straightened himself joyfully and the gloom lifted from his face. But there was fear in the streets of Jerusalem: it lurked in the archways like an unquiet shadow. There was muttering when Nehemiah rode through the streets that sank as he came near, and rose again behind him. Even on the wall there was a change: the rubbish lay in great heaps, hindering the workmen, and when the Tirshatha spoke of it, the builders said sullenly that there was no one to take it away: the work was too much for them as it was.

At last came a day that a scared messenger broke into Nehemiah's room where he sat making up his accounts. "From all sides they will be on you," he cried. "Our enemies say among themselves, 'They shall not know, neither see, till we come in the midst among them and slay them, and the work shall cease.' There is not a road to Jerusalem that they will not have taken."

Nehemiah sat gravely listening. Over and over the man repeated his tidings: he was shaking. Outside the walls Nehemiah heard a curious uneasy murmur, the sound of a great crowd that dares not speak above its breath. He went out on the steps and looked down. The street before him was crowded; workmen and rulers, women with children at their skirts, from all over Jerusalem they had gathered. The work on the wall had stopped. Men stood in knots here and there, on the fresh-laid stones, talking uneasily, or gazing, their hands above their eyes, at the sunbaked valley and the further hills. Nothing stirred in the white noon-day glare, but there was panic terror in the sunlight.

There was a sound behind Nehemiah: he turned, and saw the men of his guard, standing to arms behind him. They had scented trouble for the Tirshatha. With a gesture, Nehemiah summoned the trumpeter beside him, and in another moment the "Assembly" rang out very clear and high. The muttering in the crowd stilled suddenly. The Tirshatha stood for a moment looking down at them. Then he spake, and his voice rang no less proudly than the trumpet.

"Be ye not afraid of them," and at the 'ye' he saw their shoulders straighten: he had done well to remind them who they were. "Remember the Lord which is great and terrible, and fight for your brethren, your sons and your daughters, your wives and your houses."

There was no shout from the people, but they stood hanging on his words. "Let half of you," he went on, "go on with the work, and behind them on the wall let the other half stand to. Every man of you, whether he builds or carries burdens, let him go with his sword by his side. Moreover, the work is great and large, and we are scattered on the wall, far from one another. In what place, therefore, ye hear the sound of the trumpet, come thither all of you. Our God shall fight for us." Once again there was cheering: slowly the crowd melted, but in an hour's time the wall bristled with spears, and Jerusalem was an armed camp.

"So," wrote Nehemiah, in his journal, "we laboured in the work, and half of them held the spears from the rising of the

morning till the stars appeared. Likewise at the same time said
I unto the people, 'Let everyone with his servant lodge within
Jerusalem, that in the night they may be a guard to us, and la-
bour in the day.'"

The news came quickly to Sanballat: he took it snarling like a
dog. Day after day went by, with no glint of spears on the roads
from Samaria. None the less it was weeks before the governor
took off his clothes to sleep.

"Neither I," he wrote, "nor my brethren, nor my servants, nor
the men of the guard which followed me, none of us put off our
clothes—except," he added hastily, "that we put them off for
washing." It was like Nehemiah to remember to put that in.

EIGHT

THE work of the wall went on. There was no gap in it anywhere, except the wide empty spaces where the gates were to
be set up. Sanballat and Tobiah and Geshem the Arabian put
their heads together: then Tobiah sat down and wrote a letter,
while Sanballat sat biting his thumb, and Geshem, who was restless in ceiled houses, walked up and down the room. It was a
polite letter: greeting from the governor of Samaria to the governor of Jerusalem, and an invitation to meet for a little conversation in one of the villages of the plain of Ono. They chose Ono
because it was near the border. Nehemiah read the letter, but he
did not trouble himself to write an answer. He sent it by word
of mouth, and it sounded a little rude.

"I am doing a great work," said Nehemiah, thinking to himself
that they had little to do when they were so anxious for conversation, "and cannot come down. Why should the work cease
whilst I leave it and come down to you?"

"And I wonder," said Nehemiah to himself as he watched the
messenger go, "which of the three, Sanballat, or Tobiah, or
Geshem the Arabian, would have plunged the knife in my back
while I talked with the other two?"

It was hard to snub Sanballat, and Tobiah, and Geshem the
Arabian. They were very pressing. Four times they wrote to beg
the favour of a little conversation: and four times Nehemiah said
that he had something better to do. So the three put their heads
together and Tobiah wrote a new letter. This letter was a friendly
warning. He told Nehemiah that there was a report abroad that
he and the Jews were planning a rebellion against Babylon: that
they were building the wall to that end: and that Nehemiah himself was to be their King. That he had invited prophets to proph-

esy about him and say, "There is a King in Judah": all which
would sound very unpleasant when it was told to the King in
Babylon. So would it not be wise for Nehemiah to come and
take a little friendly advice? That letter came open in the hands
of the messenger: he showed it as his passport when he came to
the guard, and the story of what was in it had gone round the
wall before it reached Nehemiah. There were sick hearts on the
wall that day, for they had no mind to the vengeance of Babylon.

Nehemiah read the letter. It was a long letter, but his answer
was short. "Whatever story is going," he said, "is the story you
have made up yourself." The messenger went his way, and once
again Nehemiah made his rounds on the walls. He came home
with his heart a little heavy. And then he who had been strength-
ening other men's hands all day sat down and wrote in his journal
what he would have expressed to no man. "They have made us
all afraid. O God, strengthen my hands."

It was a day or two after that he went, still a little heavy at
heart, to see the house of Shemaiah the prophet. For he thought
to himself, "He is a holy man, and it may be he will have some
word from God for me." Shemaiah sat in the half light of a room
darkened, and when Nehemiah spoke he rose and looked at him
as a man doomed. Then he came forward and clutched the governor's sleeve. "Come," he said and Nehemiah felt him shaking,
"come with me into the temple, and let the doors of the temple
be shut, for no man will dare to touch you in the holy place."

Nehemiah stood still. He was no coward, but there was something abroad that shook his nerve.

"Come," went on the prophet, his voice more shrill, "for they
will come to slay thee. Yea, in the night they will come to slay
thee."

Nehemiah jerked his arm free. It was as though daylight were
about him again. "*Should such a man as I flee?*" he asked, and at
the magnificent assurance of it the prophet's mouth opened and
shut. "Who is there, being as I am," Nehemiah's head went up

and his shoulders squared, "would go into the temple to save his life? I will not go in." He turned on his heel and strode out of the dim-lit twilight room into the daylight noises of the street. "Yonder is a place for bats," he said to himself. But when he sat at his table that night and wrote the doings of the day in his journal, the meaning of that ugly scene came suddenly upon him.

"He had no vision from God," he said to himself slowly. "Sanballat and Tobiah hired him. They hired him to make me afraid, that I might hide in the temple, and they make an evil story of it." He sat for a long time. It was as though he had lifted a stone and saw the ugly things that live under it, scuttling out of the light. It made him sick. Then, with a long breath, he remembered the cleanness of God. "My God," he said to himself. Then he set his mouth and wrote the last of that day's entry. "My God, think Thou upon Tobiah"—he thought of Tobiah first, for it was Tobiah's trick: Sanballat was not cunning enough—"and Sanballat according to these their works." And then he went contented to his bed, and there came no man to kill him that night. And when Nehemiah next opened his journal this was the entry he wrote in it: "So the wall was finished in the twenty and fifth day of the month Elul, in fifty and two days." He sat for a while, looking at the page. It was September, when the earth was very still, and the harvest done. He had thought to write a long entry that night, but after all, what need was there of any more words? The wall was finished: the thing to which he had set his hand was done. "Finished," said Nehemiah to himself, and the silence of September fell upon his heart.

NINE

So the wall was finished." Nehemiah sat in his rooms in the governor's house, and looked at the words he had written twelve years ago. Once again he was governor of Jerusalem. For though he had kept his word and gone back to Babylon, to his master the King, he had wearied in its great spaces for the little city huddled on the rock, and once again he had entreated the King, and the King had given him his will. That was months ago, but the space in the journal was blank. There was not much of the great parchment left. Nehemiah sat pondering, wondering how to fill it; and as he sat, a great dejection fell upon him. "So the wall was finished": he remembered the night that he had written that, and dated it; the night that he thought his work was done. He passed on to the long entry of the day of the dedication of the wall, his great day, when the princes and the priests made the circuit of the walls, singing as they went, and trumpets blowing. Nehemiah had brought the singers from the little country villages where they had settled; for he loved music, and he was set on bringing back the great days of David and Asaph, when the Temple was famous for its singing. "The singers and the porters," he had written, "both kept the ward of their God." There was the day that Ezra the scribe stood up and read the Law, till the people wailed for their sins and the judgments of God: and at last himself rose up and said, "Go your way, eat the fat and drink the sweet, and send to the poor that have nothing prepared: neither be ye sorry, for the joy of the Lord is your strength." It was the night after that they kept the Feast of Tabernacles: he remembered how the lights twinkled out over the city at dusk, and every roof had its house of green boughs, and everywhere the sound of children laughing, till all Jerusalem was a child again. And the next day, when they came with children's hearts and vowed to keep themselves a people separate for God: to marry no worshipper of strange gods; to buy no wares from the heathen village folk on the Sabbath; to forgive all debts; and to keep up the service and the beauty of the Temple. Nehemiah had written it in his journal, with his heart saying, "O rare new world!" What city was to be like unto his city, fresh from the mercy of God?

There the journal had broken off. Nehemiah read them through, the promises, and the names of the men who had signed them. Then he began to write, and his mouth was very bitter. He wrote of his coming to Jerusalem: how he went to the great chamber in the Temple where the offerings of the people were stored, the first-fruits of the corn, the new wine and the frankincense and the oil, the great room that smelt of the open harvest fields. It was empty; instead there were rugs and rich hangings, the furnishings of the bedchamber of a prince. Might it please his Excellency, the high priest was kin to Tobiah the Ammonite, and had fitted up the room against such times as Tobiah should visit Jerusalem. The Tirshatha said nothing, but himself fell to, and in a little while the court was littered with the private belongings of Tobiah. There were many, for Tobiah loved to lie softly. "Now wash it," said Nehemiah, "and bring the holy vessels back, and the people's offerings." The holy vessels were brought back, but there were no offerings. As for the Levites and the singers, they were fled, every one to his field; no one cared for them, and they had starved in the Temple. "I contended with the rulers," so wrote Nehemiah, "and said, 'Why is the house of God forsaken?'" And the singers were brought back, and the tithes gathered in, and honourable men appointed to the treasury. Then the Sabbath came, and Jerusalem was like an open market, country people with wine and grapes and figs, and fish from Tyre, dark-skinned men from the sea with gold rings in their ears and strange curses, all these lodging in Jerusalem. This was how Jerusalem kept its word, and its Sabbaths. He turned them out, and shut the gates at dark on Saturday night, not to be opened till sunrise on Monday morning, and then they camped outside the wall, so as to tempt the people out, until Nehemiah threatened to lay hands on them.

After that, he went to a ruler's house, and spoke to his small daughter, playing in the court, and she stared at him and answered in the tongue of the Philistines. And her father laughed and said, "Her mother was from Ashdod, and the child knows no Hebrew." Nehemiah turned and hit him in the face. Was it for this he had built a wall about Jerusalem, to keep the city separate for God? Everywhere he went he heard the Philistine tongue in the streets; the grandson of the high priest was married to a daughter of Sanballat. "I chased him from me," wrote Nehemiah. "Remember them, O my God, because they have defiled the priesthood and the covenant."

The parchment was very nearly full; there was only a narrow strip left. Was it to end like this, the work that began so fair, in anger and disappointment and despair? Was it for this he had built the city of God! The light was all but gone: Nehemiah went over to the window, and saw the last slow fires of the sunset burn on the battlements of cloud. He stood there, remembering; remembering that once he saw in it Jerusalem. Well, he had seen Jerusalem; it lay below him, grey and sordid in the twilight, and still the city burned in the sunset, glorious and far. Slowly the bitterness ebbed from him. He stood silent before the vastness of the purposes of God. He had done what he could: he had built the wall of Jerusalem; but the kingdom of God is within. "*Remember me, O my God, and spare me according to the greatness of Thy mercy. Remember me, O my God.*"

So with his broken purposes, his yearning for a new heaven and a new earth wherein dwelleth righteousness, Nehemiah was joined unto the goodly fellowship, the fellowship for whom were written the two great Pilgrim Choruses of the world. *"These all died in faith, not having received the promises, but having seen them afar off."* For he looked for a city which hath foundations, whose builder and maker is God.

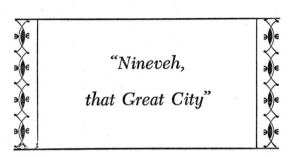

"*Nineveh,*
that Great City"

HE WAS a lean man, and he knew no Assyrian but half a dozen words. He went with his cloak wrapped about him and his head bowed; and every now and then he raised his head and cried the words he knew—"Yet forty days and Nineveh shall be overthrown." Children ran from the sight of him, and the women came to their doors, for at first they thought it might be the seller of fresh figs; but when they saw him they shrank back again. For the cry was terrible, and when he lifted his head and looked at them, the hate in his eyes was a strange thing to see. The men in the markets laughed at first—there were many markets in Nineveh, for to go from one end to the other of the city took three days. They said he was crazed; but when his eye fell on them they held their tongues. Nineveh stood about them, as solid as the earth beneath their feet. Nineveh, the greatest city in the earth, on whose walls two chariots could drive abreast—the world would come to an end as soon as Nineveh. Yet this man looked as though he had seen the end of the world. He went pacing on, as though he paced towards it, and the will that drove him was not his own. Doom had come out of the desert. Did he speak the doom of God?

He passed the palace of the King and the temples, passed the hanging gardens, and the great arsenal. The King looked down at him, and was afraid. Through the great squares he went, looking neither to the right hand nor to the left, and down into the streets and lanes, unhasting, unresting. For a whole day he paced the streets, and fear went before him and closed in behind him.

That night the King could not sleep. And he rose from his couch and he laid his robe from him and covered himself with sackcloth and sat in ashes. And in the morning there was a royal proclamation read in all the squares and open spaces. There was to be a fast for man and beast, from water and from food, even for the horses in the stable and the cows in the byre. Let every man turn from his evil way and from the violence that was in his hand, and cry mightily unto God. It might be that God would turn away from His fierce anger and relent.

The lean man had made himself a shelter of palm branches, outside the city walls. He sat there in the shadow, waiting. The second day he rose to see what had become of the city, and found it in sackcloth. He knew no Assyrian, but the signs were plain. Men repented in Nineveh as they did in Jerusalem. There was no sound of work in the streets, only a wailing from the darkened houses, and sometimes a pitiful lowing from the byres. He came back to his hut and sat there, and his heart was hot within him. It was the wickedest city in the world and the cruellest. They had tortured his own people, they had taken the whole earth captive and tortured it. And now they were going to get off. God was going to let them off. What was the good of a God with a heart as soft as that? What was the use of being good yourself, when God was as kind to bad people who said they were sorry as to you? What was the use of God liking you, if He liked people like the Assyrians too? The sun was hot on the lean man's head, but he did not care.

He wakened early the next morning and looked out through a strange screen of leaves. A vine had grown in the night, and was clambering over the paltry little shelter he had made. Very fresh and green it was; the dew was on it. Looking at it, a little of the anger died out of the lean man's heart. He watered the little tendrils of the vine clutching at the roof that he had made; like a baby's hands they were. It was so young, and so tender, and the shadow it cast was very cool.

His heart was very soft as he sat under it. After all, perhaps God had a special care for him. It was mindful of Him to grow the vine just there. The lean man sat under it all day, thinking.

His head sank on his knees. Towards evening a herd of goats passed him, driven out after milking. The small boy following them was singing. The words were strange, but the sound far off was like the song his own small brother sang, driving out the goats at home. For a moment the lean man's heart softened to the little lad. Then he remembered he was of the viper's brood. He should be killed young. If God had kept His word, he would have been.

The sun was already hot when he rose next morning. A withered leaf hung drooping from the roof of palm branches: was there a caterpillar eating it? He looked. The vine lay dead upon the roof, the little tendrils twisted like the claws of a dead bird. Just at the root a worm had cut it clean through.

The lean man raised his hands and shook them at the sky. So young it was, that vine. What was God thinking of that such things should be? What for did He make things, to let them die in a day? The sun beat down upon him pitilessly; the dead vine shrivelled under it. And the lean man said to himself, "It is better to die than to live in a world like this."

Then something spoke in his heart. Almost teasingly it spoke. "Art thou greatly angry about the vine?" The lean man held up his head fiercely. "I am greatly angry, even unto death."

There had been a faint sound of laughter in the voice before. It was grave enough now.

"Thou hadst pity on the vine," it said, "that thou hadst not made, nor taken any trouble for; that grew up in a night and died in a night. And should I not spare Nineveh, that great city, with children, thousands of them, that do not know their right hand from their left; besides much cattle?"

Jonah rose and looked at Nineveh. He saw it, but not any longer a great city, its walls flouting heaven with their strength. He saw dim little streets, with children playing at the doors, and men and women working for their children: he saw the patient cows in the byre. "And God's compassion brooding over all."

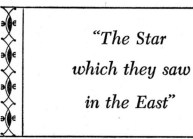

"The Star
which they saw
in the East"

U P IN the deep blue fields of air the great stars wheeled and burned. Jupiter and Saturn stood together in the House of the Fish for the first time in eight hundred years, and the glory of them lightened all that part of heaven. Twice eight hundred years after Christ was born, a man stood by his telescope in Prague, brooding over the lines and circles on the sheets before him. Night after night he watched, while Mars, the star of the war-god, burned his slow way through heaven to join his great brethren. And some time on a winter night in 1603, the three stars came together, and the patient watcher saw a thing that made his heart burn. For even as Mars came nearer, a new strange star, shining and changing like a precious stone, flamed for a while between Juipter and Saturn, and slowly went out. To this man, watching, it was as though he clasped hands across a great gulf of years with those men, wise like himself in the counsels of the stars, who had stood on the flat roof of a house in an Eastern town and watched the planets wheel and the strange star burn, and knew it for the coming of a King. Once in every eight hundred years Jupiter and Saturn come together in the House of the Fish, with Mars to follow them. That they had so come, Kepler knew, but that the strange new passing star had flamed to their eyes, even as now, he could not surely know. But he wrote of what he had seen, the wonder and the mystery of it, in a book called *De Stella Nova*; and yet another wise man laid his gift at the cradle of the King.

Now that the stars of the three gods, Jupiter, Saturn and Mars, stood together, about the time Our Lord was born, the records of the stars can show. But of the strange star there is no record, except that on the tables of the Chinese—for they, too, are in the counsels of the stars—there is mention of some such vanishing radiance as this, and at such a time; a record that is almost 2,000 years old.

There is no surety. Nor do we know the names of the Wise Men, though the Middle Ages made a rich legend of them. We do not know if they were kings or princes, nor whence they came. They come out of darkness into starlight, and go from starlight again into darkness. But in the starlight they are noble figures, the first of the great caravan of those who go in pilgrimage to find the King. The Chaldeans were stargazers always; and it may be that they came from that same plain where the first Hebrew, the man from Beyond the River, saw the sun set and the stars come out, and craved for a God who would not change and pass, and went out, not knowing whither he went, to find him. "Abraham rejoiced to see My Day," said Christ in the Temple; "he saw it and was glad." These three saw only the morning star of it; "and when they saw the star," says St. Matthew, "they rejoiced with exceeding great joy."

"See how from far upon the eastern road
The star-led wizards haste with odours sweet."

Always on the road they are, with a great dark land behind them, and the night above it brooding and mournful; but these have their faces to a star, and they are greater than men in the darkness, for they stand for the Wisdom of the world. And again in the lantern-light, kneeling, their heads bowed to the earthen floor, and their hands outstretched with their offerings to the King. There are shadows about the crib, and on their bowed heads, but the lantern light gleams on the precious things they hold. For they are the gifts that the world has brought to its King; gold, for the glory and honour of the nations; incense, for worship; myrrh, for death.

Matthew

the Publican

IT WAS late afternoon. The heat inside the little custom-house was stifling. Matthew came out and sat at the door, in the shadow, and looked down the road to the harbour. No one came or went along it: the harbour itself was deserted. One or two boats had come in that morning; Matthew knew that, for it was his business to take toll of the fish, and there had been the usual wrangle. But the wind had fallen, and they had not gone out again. One of the men had stayed on board to mend the net, and had fallen asleep, huddled upon it. Far out on the lake a few boats lay becalmed; their white sails looked like butterflies asleep. Close at hand the lake water came and went silently; there was not lapse enough to lift a pebble.

There came a sound of footfalls on the road, muffled by the thick white dust. Matthew turned to look. A lame man came down the road, leading a donkey with wine-skins slung on either side. Matthew knew the donkey and his driver; he remembered him on the roads when he was a boy at school. He sat watching, his hand shielding his eyes, until they came abreast.

"You have a good load to-day," he said.

The lame man had not seen him till he spoke. He grunted. "It is hard for the fly to get the spider asleep," he said, and spat upon the ground.

Matthew was used to it. It was all in the day's work. "It is wine that you have," he said, and reached for his tablets.

"If you could call it wine," said the lame man. Then he gleamed. "Maybe you would be for tasting it?" he urged. "I would not be grudging it to your father's son."

"Two wine-skins," said Matthew, unheeding. "The tax is a tenth on wine."

[195]

"There were two when I started," said the lame man. "But there was a leak in the far one, and the half of it is on the road from Chorazin."

"In the throats of the crowd that you met over the hill yonder," said Matthew, unmoved. "And you would charge them dear, for the half of them are south country men and know no better. Two wine-skins . . . and the market price" . . . He began to jot down figures.

"It is a dirty business," said the lame man, "and I did not think I would see your father's son in it."

Matthew was doing a sum. He seemed not to hear.

"I mind when I first was on the roads, with the mother of the little ass here," said the lame man, "it was a swine of a Gentile they had here. They couldn't have got a Jew to do their dirty work for them, then. But the spirit is out of the people since the rebellion. Though there's a man over the hill yonder—" he stopped.

"What about him?" said Matthew, lifting his head.

"Is it a spy you would be as well as a publican?" said the lame man jeering.

Matthew went back to his sum. "You needn't be telling me," he said. "I heard him myself."

"About the matter of the kingdom?"

"Yes."

"And when did you take to going to church, Matthew?" said the lame man.

"He preaches down in the harbour sometimes," said Matthew. He spoke as if he had forgotten the lame man. "He was there yesterday. He passes this way every day."

"Well, you'll not get much off *him*," said the lame man. "He has nothing but the clothes on his back. Though they say he could have whatever he liked. Maybe he could, and maybe he couldn't. But the cures of him are wonderful. He could make great money that way."

"It is not money he wants," said Matthew. "Have you got it there?"

"It's more than I can say of yourself," said the lame man. He undid the leather wallet, and counted out the coins grudgingly. "How much of that for yourself, Matthew, and how much for the cash-box?" he asked.

Matthew said nothing. The lame man eyed him curiously as he moved to the donkey's head.

"Is there anything ails you, Matthew?" he said.

"What should ail me?" said Matthew.

The lame man jerked the donkey. "Because the last time I was this way you charged me half as much again."

Matthew started. "Here!" he called, "wait!"

"You'll not get it now," said the lame man; but he stopped, curious.

"How much was it?" said Matthew. The lame man told him. Matthew counted it out and doubled it. "Here," he said.

The lame man watched him blankly. "Maybe it's repented you have," he said. "But there never was a publican repented yet." He hit the donkey, and the pair jogged on down the road.

Matthew sat down again on the doorstep. It was true. He had heard it many a time. Once a publican, always a publican. Money you had, and plenty. Yet the Man who had preached in the harbour—only yesterday they had brought a man to him lying paralysed on the broad of his back, and He said to him that his sins were forgiven him, before ever the sick man said a word. Matthew sighed. Maybe if he were sick himself, it would give him a chance. But it wasn't likely He'd have anything to say to the likes of him. He had spoken to Peter and Andrew, and taken them from the fishing; James and John, too; and them in the very boat with their father. The old man was in a great way about it, and the season just begun. That was another reason why Matthew couldn't go near Him. Peter would have put in against him; Peter knew too much about him. The Man wouldn't have anything to say to a cheat like him. Anyhow, he was too old. There'd be nothing for it but the custom-house, and the crowd, and the smell of the harbour, all his days.

There was a sudden commotion on the road. The crowd from the preaching came streaming past, men from the harbour, women with children in their arms, all hurrying to be home for supper. Matthew got up and sat in the shadow at the back of the booth. This was what he waited for every day, the moment when the Man passed by. He sat peering out of the shadow, grey and wizened, not unlike the spider that the lame man had called him; but his eyes were eager. Gradually the crowd slackened; three or four men came together. Peter and James and John, men who were always with Him; but He was not among them. He wasn't coming. There were nights that He didn't come back to the town at all, but went off to the hills by Himself, and stayed out all night. Two small boys stopped to fight in front of Matthew's booth; someone called them shrilly, and they ran on. After that no one came.

Matthew went to the door and looked up and down the road. It was empty again and quiet. He wasn't coming. Matthew went back and sat down again, and began to make up his accounts for the day. Suddenly a shadow fell across the light, and darkened the door. Matthew raised his head, and looked into the face of Christ.

He stood a while in the doorway, looking at him. "Come, Matthew," He said, and, turning, stepped into the dusty road. And Matthew rose and followed Him.

This was how Matthew found what it was to repent. And this was why, after making a great feast for the Man in his own house, and asking all his disreputable rich friends to meet Him, he left his house and his gains, to tramp the roads of Palestine. One thing only he kept—his tablets and his good clerk's hand;

and sometimes at night he wrote down what the others called "The Words." And so, long after the Man that he followed was crucified, his notes were pieced together and made into a book; and the "words" of Matthew the publican became the Gospel of Matthew the Saint.

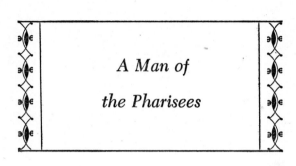

A Man of

the Pharisees

I T WAS the dark of the moon after the feast of its fullness at the Passover, which is now Easter. Out in the fields the April night was fragrant and dim, but in the narrow Jerusalem streets it was close and very dark. This was a mean little street, no better than a lane, and it climbed the hill in steps like stairs. A man came down it, slowly, holding a lantern before him. He was a big man, of a fine presence; more than that one could not see, for his cloak muffled the lower part of his face. It was plain that the way was strange to him; he went cautiously, for he was a heavy man, and once or twice he stumbled. There was no light from the houses, and most of the low doors were barred for the night. One of them opened as he went by, and two men stood on the threshold, taking leave of each other. The light streamed out on the big man as he went past, and he raised his arm as if to adjust the lantern, so that his face was in shadow. But as he did it, his cloak fell away, and they saw the spotless white of the robe below it, and the long falling fringe. The one nudged the other, and they stood silent till the sound of the footsteps was faint.

"When was a Pharisee last in this street?" asked one of them with a grin.

The other spat upon the ground. "Yon was more than a Pharisee," he said; "yon was a Judge."

"Of the Sanhedrin?"

"Aye. It was Nicodemus. I knew the step of him. He and a parcel of them were in the Temple when yon Man from Nazareth turned it inside out and miscalled it for a den of thieves. The others were for stepping out to challenge him, but I saw this one nodding them back."

"They do not like much done unless themselves are the doing of it," said the first man.

"They do not. Very cautious they are. Do you mind how they went to ask John in the desert who he was and all about him? They didn't get much out of *him*. And they'll watch this one; watch and see if they can use him. And if he gives any trouble—"

"Whist," said the other. A door farther up the street had opened. They saw the tall figure of the man who had passed them standing at it. He seemed to be asking a question. Then he stooped his head and passed in, and the door was shut.

"That's where he lodges," said the man of the house.

"Who?"

"Him we were talking about. He'll have come to find out all about him. Wouldn't come in the daytime. They're too big for that." And again he spat on the ground, and they said, "Good night."

Meanwhile, Nicodemus was stumbling up a flight of uneven stairs. The man who had opened the door went before him. He had answered Nicodemus' question about this being the lodging of Jesus of Nazareth in the up-country brogue; Nicodemus supposed he was one of the men who had come with the new preacher from Galilee.

A door opened, and he found himself in a low-ceiled upper room. A single candle burned on the table, its flame steady in the closeness of the night. The man he had come to see was standing by the open window. He turned as Nicodemus came in, and made him gravely welcome, so little surprised by a visitor so late that Nicodemus' apology tailed off into silence.

Nicodemus had prepared what he would say, for he was a shy man. The man in the street was wrong; he had not come as a spy from the Sanhedrin, the Supreme Court of Judges, which even the Romans recognised, and to which they had left the power of all but death. Why he came, he hardly knew himself. They would lift their eyebrows, the men who were his friends. They had talked a good deal about the new preacher, dining in one another's houses. Sometimes they stopped on the fringe of the crowd when he preached in the street, and would nod approval before they passed on. He was an extremist, of course, but he was young, and so far he had said nothing that anyone could take exception to. And the cures he had performed were certainly miraculous. He had a great influence with the common people. Quite possibly in the providence of God he had been sent to call the crowds to repentance: undoubtedly there was need enough of that. Not the kind of man one would ask to one's house, of course. He went about with the most impossible people, one of them actually an ex-publican. All this Nicodemus had heard; it was part of the reason why he came by night. But there was another reason too. It was not only over the crowds that this man had power. The thought of him came between Nicodemus and his books; it came into his ordered scholar's life and troubled it. His life had stretched before him like a quiet, dignified street with the houses of his friends on either side, a street down which he would pace, stately and honoured, to the end. He was middle-aged; a Judge of the Supreme Court; he had succeeded in life. And suddenly restlessness had come upon him; the long debates were savourless to him. It reminded him of the days when he was a young man, and sitting late at his books, and the smell of new-mown hay would drift through his window above all the curious warm smells of the Jerusalem streets, and he would wonder for a moment if it would not be better to work with one's hands in the open fields than be a scholar. It was thirty years since he had felt it. He was fifty now, and his hair was growing grey. And because of the foolishness of it he kept his secret close, and came by night.

Now he was face to face with the man who had troubled his thoughts, Nicodemus stood looking at him, recalling the speech he had prepared.

"Rabbi," he began at last, though the man before him was younger than he by twenty years, "we know that thou art a teacher come from God." Even at the last he could not bring himself to speak for himself alone. That was why he took refuge in the "we." He paused. The Rabbi made no acknowledgment of the compliment, but his eyes searched Nicodemus, waiting, questioning. Nicodemus blundered heavily into explanation.

"We have seen the miracles. No man could do those miracles unless God were with him."

There was a long silence. The Rabbi had looked away, almost in disappointment. Nicodemus sat, angry with himself. He had not said what he wanted to say. He could not get it out. At last the Rabbi spoke.

"Verily, verily, I say unto thee," he said slowly, "except a man be born again, he cannot see the kingdom of God."

Nicodemus started. Strangely, in riddles, this man was answering the thought that was in his heart. Not the sight of miracles; they did not matter: the sight of the kingdom of God. But how? Nicodemus plunged again foolishly.

"How can a man be born when he is old?" he said; and his voice was wistful as well as puzzled. Whatever the Rabbi meant by being born again, there was not much hope of a new thing for a man over fifty.

"Verily, verily, I say unto thee," said the Rabbi, again, "except a man be born of water and of the spirit, he cannot enter into the kingdom of God. That which is born of the flesh is flesh, and that which is born of the spirit is spirit."

Nicodemus sat silent. So it would be no use to a man if he could be born again. It would be the same man, born into the same world, the old noises, the old hunger, the old ways. But to be born of the spirit: how might such a thing be?

The silence deepened in the room; and the closeness of the night in that narrow street seemed to gather and hem them in. Nicodemus sat with his head sunk. He saw no way out. Suddenly the Rabbi raised his head. Nicodemus roused himself to listen.

They heard it a great way off. It came nearer, a whisper and a sighing about the house, a strange stirring in the dead air. A

breath of wind drifted through the open window; the flame of
the candle flickered high and sank. For a moment the sense of
far spaces was in the room. It passed, and they heard it go
sounding on its fathomless way.

*"The wind bloweth where it listeth, and thou hearest the sound
thereof, but canst not tell whence it cometh and whither it goeth:
so is every one that is born of the Spirit."*

The voice ceased; but Nicodemus did not stir. For a moment
he saw it, the world that lay about his own. It was as though he
had his head for a moment above the water in which his life lay
drowned. It shut him in so close, the world that he saw and
heard; it lay like a weight of water when he moved. Now for a
moment he was free of it; free in this strange clear world, where
the wind was the breath of God.

Hours after, Nicodemus was again in the sleeping streets. He
went like a man walking in his sleep. Strange words rang in his
ears, fragments of mysteries too great for any man's understanding. He groped among the hidden bases of the hills, but somewhere, he knew, they lifted their heads into the freshness of the
eternal world, the world from which this man came, to which he
would some day go. But after what horror of great darkness?
"So must the Son of Man be lifted up," he had said, and Nicodemus, listening, had felt the coldness creep about his heart. The
night was changing about him; the unearthly blue of dawn was
in the streets. But the day had not yet broken; and as he walked
he was afraid.

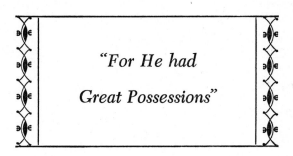

"*For He had*

Great Possessions"

THE spring rains were over in the Jordan valley: in another fortnight the barley harvest would begin. It rippled, acres of it, from the terrace where their owner stood, down to the valley road, already white with dust in a world of ripening grain. The April sunlight poured down into the valley, and the air was like the clear water in the brook.

The man who owned most of the valley stood looking down upon it, drawing long breaths. The dew on the grass had drenched his sandals. He had trodden on a sprig of wild thyme, and the sudden sharp sweetness of it seemed to put an edge on the intolerable beauty of the world. It had pierced his very brain. The earth ached with life; his own heart ached with it. Sometimes when he was a boy, and that aching came upon him, he had flung himself on the warm grass, clutching it with his hands, burying his face in it, that the earth-life might flow through him and fill that emptiness. But he was past that now. It had strengthened with his strength, that craving for he did not know what.

Once when he was reading the Roll in the synagogue—he was ruler of the synagogue, because they set his great position over against his youth—he had come on something in the Psalms that he knew: "As the hart panteth after the water brooks, so panteth my soul after Thee." Whoever wrote that had felt what he felt. Only, for himself, it was not God that he wanted. God, he dimly felt, was somewhere behind the Law. He read in the Law every day; he knew by heart the cxix Psalm, praising it; he supposed he ought to feel like that, about it. And when he thought of God, he thought of parchment, and a scroll of rules, about the Sabbath, and one's duty to one's neighbour. The man who wrote that Psalm wanted God; for himself, he wanted life. He had had thirty years of it, wealth and honour and marriage and friends, and he was thirsty still.

Just of late there had come a strange word to his ears—"eternal life": a fragment of the preaching of the new prophet from Galilee. Eternal was the word you used for God; it was bigger even than everlasting, for you sometimes spoke of the everlasting hills. It sounded great enough even to satisfy him. The servants had told him last night that the prophet was staying in the village. That very day he would go to Him and ask Him what it meant.

He stood at the end of the terrace, idly watching the road winding far below him. Round the shoulder of the hill came a solitary figure, walking alone. A moment after, came a straggling company of men, walking in twos and threes. It was strange to see so many on the road; it was too early in the month for the Passover crowds. Something about the solitary figure in front held him. It must be the Prophet. He was on the road to the ford; then He must be for Jerusalem. And He might never come this way again. The young ruler made up his mind with a rush. There was a footpath through the fields that struck the road just above the ford. If he hurried he would be just in time.

So it was that in a little while the straggling following of men saw a young man running at full speed, and stood to watch his coming. His pace slackened as he neared the foremost figure. Another moment, and he was on his knees in the dusty road. The disciples came a little nearer, sympathetic and curious. His wife at the point of death, perhaps; perhaps a baby son. For himself he could want nothing; he was in too good health for that.

"Good Master," the words came clearly, "what good thing shall I do that I may have eternal life?"

The Rabbi stood, looking down at him.

"Why callest thou Me good?" he asked. The Rabbi did not like politeness when it meant nothing. "If thou wilt enter into life" —the young man's face brightened; this was what he wanted, life that one could enter into, like the river—"keep the commandments."

The young ruler's face fell. Back to the parchment and the scroll of rules. Was the way of life through the Ten Commandments? "Which?" he asked, a little dulled.

"Thou shalt do no murder, Thou shalt not commit adultery. Thou shalt not steal, Thou shalt not bear false witness." The young man's head went proudly up. "Honour thy father and thy mother." Had they not died blessing him? "Thou shalt love thy neighbour as thyself." Surely he did. Never, to his knowledge, had he done an unkindness.

He looked at the Rabbi, doubtfully, wistfully. He had done all this, and it had made no difference.

"Master," he said, and his voice was a little aggrieved, "all these have I kept from my youth up. What lack I yet?"

There was a long silence. The Rabbi stood, looking down into the young man's face. Peter, watching, saw a look come into his Master's eyes, and felt a sudden stound of jealousy. Already He loved him; loved him perhaps as much as He did Peter, who had given up everything for Him. And this man—Peter's eye fell on the richness of the cloak trailing in the dust—this man had so much already. Peter drew a step nearer, listening.

Still the Rabbi gazed. So honourable a face it was, and so eager. So wide, in its desire, so narrow in the life it knew. It rolled like a map, that life, before the eyes of the shabby young Rabbi on the road, so easy a life, so prosperous, so comfortable and kindly, with a wall growing higher each year round the solitary soul. If only he would come out and leave it all behind him; use that great wealth of his not any more for his own pleasure, but to save other men from pain. Not to give up, but to give away. And so to find the everlasting habitations, the love of men's hearts, the love of God.

"One thing thou lackest. If thou wilt be perfect, go and sell that thou hast and give to the poor, and thou shalt have treasure in heaven." The voice lost its note of sternness: it no longer said "Go." "And come, and follow Me."

The head before Him was bowed. Apart from the eyes where he might have read the promise of the life that was to be, the ruler's eyes fastened on the dust of the road. Eternal life—was this eternal life, to empty one's self, to spend one's self for naught? He wanted something to make life rich. This man asked him to make it poor. Slowly he rose, his eyes still fixed on the ground, and slowly he turned away.

Brightness had fallen from the air. What ailed him he did not know, though one, years after, could have told him. Like Paul, he had seen the Lord Christ, and it was hard for him to kick against the pricks. He had seen the Lord Christ; and though he was not to count all things but loss that he might win Him, he was to find that all things were loss without Him.

The Rabbi stood a long time, looking after him. "With men, this is impossible, but with God all things are possible." He said it, and again took the road.

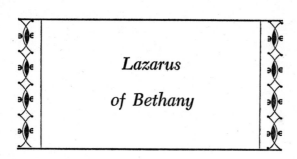

Lazarus

of Bethany

THE road from Bethany slipped down into the valley. It was steep, for Bethany lies high on the shoulder of the hill, and a tricklet of water by the roadside, swollen with the rains, went swiftly, talking to itself. Half-way down the hill a goat-track struck the road. It led to the fields above Bethany, and a woman had come down by it, and was standing on the grass at the edge of the road. She did not want to come out into the village street; she had gone out through the garden at the back of her house, and down by the path through the fields. Now she stood with her hand shading her eyes, watching the far-off winding of the road. The sunlight was soft, but her eyes ached with crying, and she had not slept. She was dry-eyed now; she did not think that she would ever cry any more. He had been dead four days. Nothing would make any difference, now.

She had thought she was used to his being dead. There was no other thought in the dark house she had left, with her sister sitting with her hands in her lap looking straight before her, and the neighbour women coming in and out and crying easily when they spoke of him. But now that she had come out alone into the soft young air, it was as though she had never known it until now. The blue overhead was so gentle; it was as though the sky bent above the earth, loving it. The young green of the trees clung about the hills like a mist; was there anything on earth so tender as the buds on the spines of the thorn? In their own garden as she came through it the almond tree was in blossom. She had broken down when she saw it, shaking with sore angry sobs and no tears, like a wind that has no rain. To be dead, when the very grass at her feet was living, and a tiny green beetle walked on it and swung in a sort of trance of joy. To be dead, hidden away out of it all in a dark cave on the face of the hill with a stone across the mouth of it, and the cold stone under his head, he that was like a young tree, growing in the light. In the dark house it was for herself that she had grieved; out here it was for him.

They were in sight at last, a little cluster of moving figures that she would have given her heart to see four days ago. She had come out here the morning of the day that Lazarus died, and sent her soul out across the valley to the far blue hills with such an agony of longing as might have brought the very hills more near. And He had not come. He was coming now; always in front, walking with the tireless step, unhasting, unresting, of one always on the roads. He could come now; now when it was too late. And how Lazarus had loved Him. He would have died for Him. Nothing in the house was too good for Him when He came. And He had let him die without Him, when a word would have saved him. Struggling with herself she went slowly, step by step, down the road. He saw her, and came to meet her, and as she lifted her eyes the anger fell from her, and left only one great ache of pain.

"Lord," she said, for the old word rose to her lips in spite of herself, "if Thou hadst been here, my brother had not died."

There was silence for a while. Then the familiar voice spoke, briefly, almost coldly.

"Thy brother shall rise again."

That was all. Had He come a day's journey to tell her what the scribes could tell her every Sabbath, what every relation who had come to the house this last horrible four days had told her? What did she care about the resurrection, hundreds of years away? She wanted him living, living now.

"I know," she said dully, "that he shall rise again at the resurrection at the Last Day."

She had turned away from Him; her eyes were on a young blue butterfly, dancing across the green wheat.

"I am the resurrection and the life: he that believeth in Me, though he were dead, yet shall he live; and whosoever liveth and believeth in Me shall never die. Believest Thou this?"

It was His voice, but the life of the whole world was in it, the tenderness of the sky above the earth, the silent breathing of the trees. Could there be death on earth, with that Presence in it?

"Yea, Lord," she answered, and the assurance of it came up about her heart. The cave on the hill was empty. Somewhere in the sunlight, Lazarus walked and was glad.

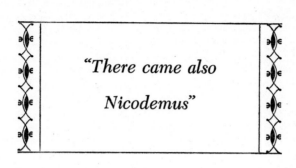

"There came also Nicodemus"

It WAS growing dark as Pilate left the Judgment Hall, and passed down the corridor to his own apartments in the Palace. The lights were not yet lit, and the April moon rode high above the courtyard. The corridor was open along one side, and the pillars cast deep black shadows on the floor. Pilate went swiftly, and frowning. It had been a vexatious day. For the thousandth time since he left Rome, with the lictors pacing before him, he cursed the fate that had made him Procurator of Judaea. A cantankerous lot they were, canting hypocrites: hounding an innocent man to death in the morning, and then begging to have him cut down, lest his body should hang on the cross over the Sabbath, and so break one of their paltry little laws. "Straining at gnats and swallowing camels"—it was the man they killed today who had said it of them, and set all Jerusalem laughing. No wonder they hated him. Anyhow, Pilate had galled them with the title he had written for the cross—"Jesus of Nazareth, King of the Jews." Pilate chuckled grimly to himself, but the chuckle ended in a half-groan. This morning's work haunted him. The man was innocent. But there would have been a riot if he had refused to crucify him. For a while the mob looked very ugly. And there were complaints enough in Rome already without that. Pilate glanced out into the moonlight; nine o'clock this morning; it would not be over yet. Well—Pilate shrugged his shoulders, a shrug that was half a shudder. The sooner one had a bath and dinner, the sooner to drink and forget—if a man could get drunk on the stuff they called wine here!

The door of the Judgment Hall opened suddenly, and Pilate started. Something had played havoc with his nerves. It was one of his own lictors.

"Sir," he said, "one of the Sanhedrin to speak with you."

In his relief Pilate swore the roundest oath he knew. "Have I not been polluted all day with the dogs?" he shouted. "Twice already have they been back, since the whole bandog crew of them came yelping this morning. Which of them is it now?"

"It is Joseph of Arimathea," said the lictor. Pilate hesitated, and his anger cooled. Joseph of Arimathea was rich, and he was powerful; an honourable man, too, not like those two-faced knaves of high priests, Annas and his son-in-law. And the time was coming when Pilate might be glad of the good word of one of the provincials he governed. He turned and went back to the Praetorium, standing a moment in the doorway before he passed through. Joseph of Arimathea stood in the midst of the hall, gazing slowly round it. His eye wandered from the Judgment seat to where the prisoner must have stood that morning, and Pilate wondered at the dumb anguish on his face. He stepped forward and greeted him.

"I have come to ask a boon," said Joseph. "It is concerning Jesus of Nazareth."

"He was crucified this morning," said Pilate briefly.

"I know it. I have come to ask his body for burial."

Pilate looked at him. He had not known that the man had friends so powerful.

"But you are of the Sanhedrin?"

"I was."

"And now?"

"I am a disciple of Jesus of Nazareth."

Pilate looked perplexed. Not two days ago he had heard Joseph of Arimathea spoken of as one of the chiefs of the Council. "I did not know it," he said at last.

"No man knew it. I was afraid."

"Not now?"

"Not now."

There fell a silence. Pilate moved uneasily. "It is your wish to have him for burial? But he cannot be dead yet. It was only this morning—"

"He is dead," said Joseph heavily.

Pilate turned and spoke to the lictor waiting in the shadow at the door. The man went out, and in a little while came back with the centurion.

"The man you crucified this morning—is he yet alive?" The centurion saluted.

"Dead, sir, at the ninth hour."

"How long after—?"

"Six hours."

The perplexed frown gathered deeper on Pilate's forehead. "Lights there!" he ordered. They brought in torches, and he wrote an order, sealed it, and handed it to the waiting Councillor. Joseph of Arimathea took it, bowed, and passed out. Pilate stood and watched him go. Was the world turned upside down? The folly of it, when he had kept his secret so long, to lose the world for it now. To lose the world to give a dead man decent burial—for a dream's sake. Slowly he turned and went out, shaken and half-sick. He had seen a thing that was too high for him, and for a moment he felt the contraction of the heart that comes upon a man looking at a dizzy height.

In the dark of the archway leading to the street, Joseph of Arimathea, passing out, stumbled against a man coming in. He halted to apologise, with ceremony. Then he saw the man's face, plain in the moonlight, and the courtly words went from him.

"Nicodemus!" he cried.

The older man lifted his head, and looked him in the face.

"I am come to ask Pilate for the body of Jesus of Nazareth," he said steadily.

Joseph of Arimathea stood, dazed. Nicodemus, the shy, middle-aged scholar; silent, set in his ways, old before his time.

"You? But I did not know—"

Nicodemus faced him unfalteringly. "I went to Him by night

three years ago," he said. He stood a moment, looking down the moon-lit street. "It has taken three years," he added, as if to himself. He seemed to have forgotten to whom he spoke.

"I, too," said Joseph of Arimathea.

Nicodemus nodded. He had the air of one who will be surprised at nothing in this world any more. The wind that had lifted his heart that night, that for three years had not ceased to stir and sway about his life, had that day broken upon him in tempest, and now was still. It had gone out to sea.

"I must speak with Pilate," he said quietly, and made to go past.

"It was my own errand," said Joseph of Arimathea. "This is the order." He held out the scrap of parchment, with the seal. Nicodemus looked at it blankly.

"I have a garden there," went on Joseph, explaining, "and a new tomb in the rock. Never man was laid in it yet."

Nicodemus handed back the parchment and turned away. So he was too late, even to bury Him. Then he halted. "But the linen, and the spices?" he said wistfully.

Joseph went over to him, with sudden kindliness. "Do you buy those," he said. "Come, and we both will bury Him." And the two went out together.

"*A Young Man,*
whose
Name was Saul"

THE evening sacrifice was over. The smoke still went slowly up from the altar, but the priests were gone for their evening meal. The courts were almost empty: outside the pedlars and the money changers were packing up their booths and preparing to trundle them away. They were talking loudly and cheerfully, but the sound came very faintly to the inner court, where Saul of Tarsus stood at his prayers. He had come in an hour ago; passing through the grating with the notice upon it that forbade the uncircumcised to enter upon pain of death. There was a weight upon his spirit, and it had not lessened. Why he had come there, he hardly knew. Except that his heart was sick for the sound of the chanting, and the smell of the incense, and the beauty that had spoken to him of holiness ever since he first came there, a raw schoolboy from the provinces. All through his college days he had come here to worship: every stone of the marble pavement he knew. And after college, when Saul of Tarsus was already at thirty a judge of the Supreme Court, he had come, a little conscious of his youth and his position, among the white-bearded men who were his fellows. To-day as he came through the outer court, two of the booth keepers had nudged each other, and one had spat upon the ground. He had seen them do that when Stephen came through, three years ago, before they took him. Over there in the Court of Stone they had judged him, before they led him away to his death. Stephen; Stephen. The old pain surged again about Saul's heart. Would that wound never heal? Though there were worse things to remember than Stephen's face. There was the face of the man they had brought before him, after scourging, to recant. He had said after Saul the words of recantation, had cursed Jesus of Nazareth for a blasphemer and an impostor. Saul's hands twisted together. Was he never to be free? To the end of his days would that knife turn in his heart? It might have happened yesterday. "O Lamb of God that takest away the sins of the world, have mercy upon us." He had had mercy. It might be that this very agony was His mercy too: but there were days when it seemed more than Saul could bear.

> "With them into God's house I went,
> With voice of joy and praise,
> Even with the multitude that kept
> The solemn holy days."

For a moment Saul's mind flashed back, almost wistfully, to the old untroubled days, when his way had lain so straight before him, when he had stood here and thanked God for his name and race, his self-control and his honour, when his thoughts went up with the sunlight on them in praise of a God made in Saul's own image. Well, he had seen Him since. "Wherefore I do abhor myself, and repent in dust and ashes."

Some things, at least, he had saved out of the shipwreck of his pride. That keen brain, the swordplay of his wit, his merciless logic, his knowledge of the Law—they would taste the edge of it yet, these men who had made a mock of his Lord. Out of their own Scriptures would he condemn them. As for Peter and James and that silent John—they were better men than he, but they were not scholars: they had not Saul's traditions. No wonder that they had made little impression on the learned men of Jerusalem. Not until Saul came back had he realised how hungry he had been for the curial speech, for the clash of dialectic: in the first crash of debate he felt himself again a swimmer in strong familiar seas. Already, he knew, he had kindled more fury in the synagogues than Peter and the rest in three years. Fury: but was not that very fury a sign of his efficacy? And the end? Martyrdom perhaps, and a fitting expiation, if Stephen's slayer might atone for Stephen's death. But surely, in the strategy of God, who so fit to convert Jerusalem as Saul the Persecutor?

Yet still the oppression deepened upon Saul. Twilight had fallen: he was solitary and the silence of the court closed round about him, shutting him off from all the kindly life that was beyond those walls. Loneliness came upon him, a worse loneliness than he had felt since that awful solitude in Damascus, when he had lain for three days, dark at noon. Three days, until he heard the blessed feet coming through the doorway, pausing at last by his side. Even as those footsteps were coming now. So strong was the memory upon Saul that he turned, half expecting to see again the kindly venerable face that had looked down upon him and blessed him. But it was not Ananias. It was the Lord Christ.

"Make haste," He said, "and get thee quickly out of Jerusalem; for they will not receive thy testimony concerning Me."

Saul was on his knees, pleading for his life. "Lord," he urged, "they know that I imprisoned and beat in every synagogue them that believed on Thee, and when the blood of Thy martyr Stephen was shed, I was standing by and consenting unto his death, and kept the raiment of them that slew him—"

The words died. Christ had turned from him, was gazing through the open archway, past the grating with the notice on it, into the night outside.

"Depart," He said, "for I will send thee far hence unto the Gentiles."

Silently Saul rose, and went out, under the archway, past the grating. At the top of the steps he paused. What compulsion was this that had driven him out, without leave-taking, without a word of blessing to heal his hurt? He turned to come back, but the temple was empty. Empty, as Saul's own heart. He had heard sentence of banishment, sentence of death, death to his hopes, his scholarship, his ambition. Banishment from the streets that were like the veins of his body, from the Temple that was his heart. What had he to bring to the Gentiles to whom the Sacred Books were hardly a name, and all that vast argosy of learning, the very Ark of God, no better than a derelict half sunk? Nothing but—Saul's heart stood still. Nothing but the Christ that he had that moment seen. He stood on the steps of the Temple, face to face with the blue vault of heaven with its stars, Jerusalem a huddle of lights at his feet, and the uttermost horizon seemed too narrow for the tides that swept about his heart.

"God forbid that I should glory save in the cross of Christ Jesus my Lord, through whom the world is crucified unto me and I unto the world."

*"After these things
Paul . . . came
to Corinth"*

It WAS very quiet in the house of Justus; the only house in Corinth that was quiet that night. For it was May, and the third day of the Isthmian games was over. While they lasted, Corinth never went to bed. Paul stood by the window of the house of Justus, looking out. He had tried to sleep, but the closeness of the night and the sound of flutes and the footsteps ceaselessly passing drove him into a fever. It was between twelve and one, but the crowds in the streets had hardly lessened. For that matter, he was too tired to sleep. All day he had haunted the outskirts of the racecourse along with the snake-charmers, and the fortune-tellers, and the sellers of images, and the men with wine-skins; these did great business, for watching the races was thirsty work, with the early summer sun burning his way through the blue fields of the sky. Justus had warned Paul to keep in the house, for Corinth was no place for a decent man during the days of the Games; but there was no holding Paul. For one week it seemed to him the whole world was met together in Corinth, and he must preach. Necessity burnt him; yet he had hardly opened his mouth all day. He was a shy man; once or twice he had got into conversation with some strangers, and then a fresh burst of cheering shook the hot air, and the crowd would surge forward to get a look at the winner, and bet on the next race. The very children were betting. Paul had come home, silent and sunken. He stood now with the night not yet dark about him, watching the terrible streets. Across the way the torches burned before a house, and the flutes played maddeningly; there was a feast going on there. A man had dropped on the pavement outside it, dead or drunk: Corinth neither knew nor cared. A party of dancing girls passed in, the torchlight flaming on their wild faces. Paul looked down and shuddered. They were, indeed, the children of their gods, and their gods were devils. What chance had his word against a world like this?

Someone was burning spices. The sweet, heavy breath spread through the night, and the smell of wine from where a skin had burst in the street. At the end of the street the water of the harbour lapped, black and evil, on the landing stage; the harbour that made Corinth the market of the world. It was so far off, the Palestine where the Man he preached had lived and died; the little country of hill-roads and green pastures where He had spent his days in footsore journeying, the Holy City where they crucified Him. It was easy to preach Him in Jerusalem where men knew the story, where they had loved Him or hated Him. But here, where no one cared, where His very name had to be translated, to speak of Him here among their thousand gods, wealth that the Man of Nazareth had never seen, sins of which His holiness had never dreamed—it was to preach a shadow, from a quiet world of shadows. This was the real world, with its madness of flutes and cymbals, where the torches flared all night, where the night never came. So strong a world, and one man against it, with only a memory and a hope. So poor a man, too. Paul's head sank on his breast.

For a long time he stood, and the silence in the room grew. A strange quiet fell on him. Outside the torches still flared, the flutes still maddened the night, but the throbbing in his head had stopped. Paul raised his head with a long sigh, and saw the Lord Christ. He stood at the window, grey in the shadow, looking out at the street; and the torchlight flickered on His quiet face as it might flicker on heaven with its stars. He looked at the street below him, but it seemed to Paul that He saw Corinth, and beyond Corinth the illimitable reaches of the world. Not bitterly, not sorrowfully, but as a man looks at that which will some day be his.

"Be not afraid, Paul," He said at last, as though He answered the long night's distress. "Speak, and hold not thy peace. For I am with Thee." He still stood, looking out. "I have much people in this city," He said, and so passed out.

A long while after, Paul rose and stood again by the window. The torches were burning low, but the flutes still quickened, and Paul heard a new thing in them, the weariness of the players, jerking their hearts out for their daily bread. All the noises of Corinth rose about his ears, the strange mournfulness of a city that is making merry. And it seemed to him that they blended into one great cry. "O God, Thou art our Father. We are the clay, and thou our Potter, and we all are the work of Thy hand. Be not wroth very sore, O our God." He stood, stretching out his hands, his heart breaking. Children of devils? Nay rather, children of God.

"After two years,
Felix . . . left
Paul bound"

THERE was one window in the guardroom at Caesarea from which one could get a glimpse of the sea. Paul had found that out. It looked into the courtyard, but beyond the angle of the great wall there was a flash of blue flecked with white, and the sun shining on the end of the great breakwater that made the only safe harbour on that coast, and now and then the sway and dip of a white sail passing out. But the soldiers did not like that window; they found it dull. The other windows looked into the street, and they liked to hang out of them and make bets on how many cats would walk past before the relieving of the guard, and whether they would see an uglier woman than the wife of Matthew the water-carrier in one whole day. And as Paul's right hand was chained to a soldier's left, their whereabouts were also his, so that he could not look out to sea as often as he could have wished. All the same, they liked Paul, and now and then they would humour him. But in winter that window was far from the fire.

"The sea is closed, little Paul," they would argue with him, watching the stooped, silent figure at the window. "You could not go even if you were free to-morrow. Come and sit by the fire, and tell us about the shipwreck you were in. The third one. I doubt you are not a lucky person to have on board, little Paul. Shipwrecked a fourth time you would be if you were out on the sea that day. Bring him along, Julius." And Julius would come across the room to the fire, the man at the end of the chain following with a limp.

"Is your knee stiff to-day, little Paul?"

"It is so," said Paul. "I doubt it will be wet by the ache in it."

"What was it lamed you? You never told us that yet."

"A stone," said Paul briefly.

"Who threw it?"

"It was at Lystra. They threw me out of the city, and left me for dead."

"They are a fierce lot, the mountainy men," said Julius, kicking a log on the fire.

"It was not the mountainy men," said Paul. "It was my own people."

"You and they had had the queer dust," said the man who had spoken first. "It is a terrible spite they have at you, little Paul."

"It is all that," said Paul mournfully. He was thinking of the faces he had seen in the crowd below him when he stood on the steps of the Tower Antonia longing to speak, and they shrieking at him and throwing dust into the air. It was the most horrible thing he had ever seen. He saw it sometimes even yet, in his sleep, and had wakened the soldier beside him with his moaning.

"And what for you couldn't stay away from them when you had the chance?" said the man at the fire meditatively. "It was putting your head in the crocodile's jaw and saying 'Bite.' You have not much sense, little Paul."

"I have not," said Paul sadly. He sat at the end of the form, gazing back at the darkening window. The sea was grey to-day, with foam on the necks of the waves. It was a year and seven months to-day since he had seen it first from that same window, very gay in the Easter sunlight. A fortnight at most, he had said to himself, and he would be on it. Rome first, and then, perhaps, Spain. Another Easter had come, and still he looked through the guardroom window. Spring and summer and autumn, and now it was winter again. It was as though the water had closed over his head. They had all forgotten him; it was only his heart that ached as of old. At first when the news of his captivity was fresh, there had been letters and presents and visitors every day. They were proud of him, their martyr, their father in God. But there was to be no martyrdom, it appeared; simply detention at the governor's pleasure. His friends could not hang on in Caesarea for ever. He knew that; he even urged them to go, and when they had gone he was lonely as only Paul could be. They had taken him for granted even in the guardroom; they petted him as if he were a favourite old asthmatic terrier. After a while it became a game with them when Paul was sent for to interview the governor, to dice on the chances of his trial coming off at last. But it had happened so often, a dispirited Paul limping slowly back, that no one would take the odds, and Paul's heart sank a little lower.

"It's a little money he wants, Paul," they counselled him sagely. "Her ladyship is a terrible expense to him. Write to some of those grand friends of yours who came to see you at the first."

Paul shook his head, and the guardroom said what it thought of the meanness of Paul's friends.

"It is not that," said Paul. "I believe they would give me their own selves." He said it valiantly, to drown the small forlorn chill that had crept about his heart. "But I will not bribe the law."

Then the guardroom cursed the law, and cursed Paul for a fool, and brought him in an enormous cheese for his supper. And Paul lay awake listening to the peaceful snoring of the soldier chained to him on his right side, with his heart and his hope dead. Somewhere outside the moon made a shining path on the sea—the sea that would never know Paul more. The world could do without him. The churches he had fathered could do without him. Someone else would strike out West, to the Gates of Spain and the sunset. And he would grow old in the guardroom, like an old dog kennelled at last, a little greyer, a little stiffer. Soon he would be quite blind.

It lasted for two years. It is the blind alley in Paul's life. There is no record of it; no letters have been kept that were written from Caesarea. It may be that none were written.

And the end?

*"Why else was the pause prolonged but that singing might is-
sue thence?"*

Between the first group of the letters and the last there is a
great gulf. The difference between the Epistle to the Romans and
the Epistle to the Philippians is the difference between the trumpet and the violin. The man who wrote to the Churches at Ephe-
sus and Colossae and Philippi had spent two years at Caesarea,
breaking his heart upon the will of God.